BORN AGAIN

THE JOURNEY BEGINS

ONE MAN'S WALK WITH GOD

L. BRIEN ELVINS

To order additional books:
www.amazon.com
www.bornagainthejourneybegins.com

ISBN: 978-1-952943-70-6

Editorial and Book Packaging: Inspira Literary Solutions, Gig Harbor, Washington

Printed in the USA

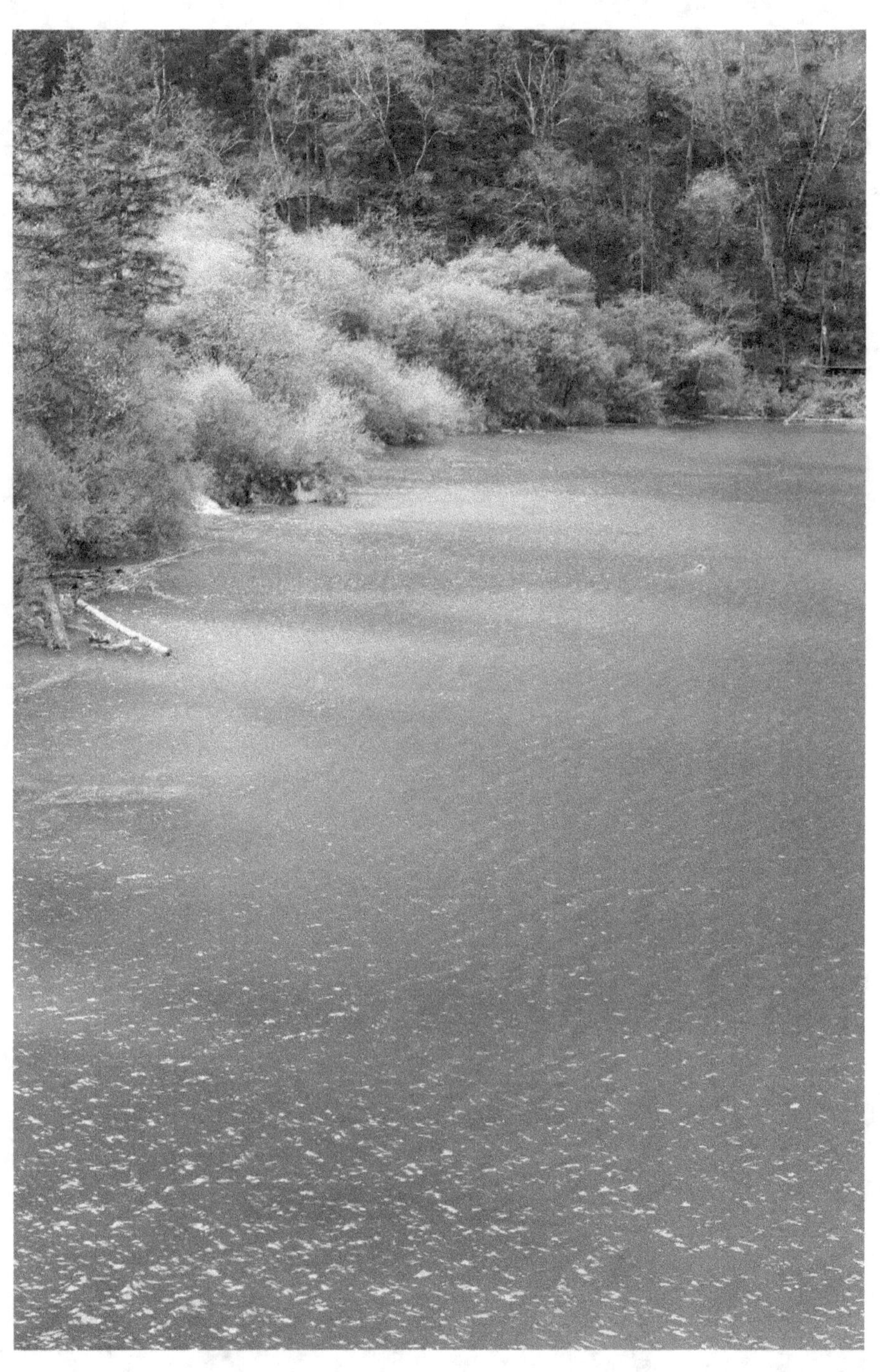

DEDICATION

Life is hard. I believe this is the way God designed it to be. If life were easy, we would not need God in our lives.

Everyone has their own personal struggles in life, Christians and non-Christians alike. But when we have God, Jesus Christ as our Lord and Savior, and the Holy Spirit, the full power of the Trinity helping us through the difficult times.

With this in mind, I would first like to dedicate this book to everyone's "life struggles."

If you are a Christian, I hope this book helps you to further build your relationship with Jesus Christ. It is *your* journey and *your* walk. If you are not a Christian, I hope this book helps you come to God, making Jesus Christ your Lord and Savior.

I would also like to dedicate this book to the past, current, and future participants and staff at Truly Motivational Transitional Living. The staff are amazing coaches and friends to the participants who struggle with alcohol and drug addiction. Truly Motivational Transitional Living provides a connection for each and every one of the individuals in the program who are healing and building their relationship with our Lord Jesus Christ. Each individual who passes through this organization is a miracle and the staff are the working hands of God, assisting Him as He heals the lives of the hurting. The participants and staff are an inspiration.

Truly Motivational Transitional Living is *TRULY SAVING LIVES,* and I am humbled by the privilege of being a Board Member.

A portion of the proceeds from this book goes to support TMTL.
If you would like to learn more or donate to their work, you can find them at tmtl.org.

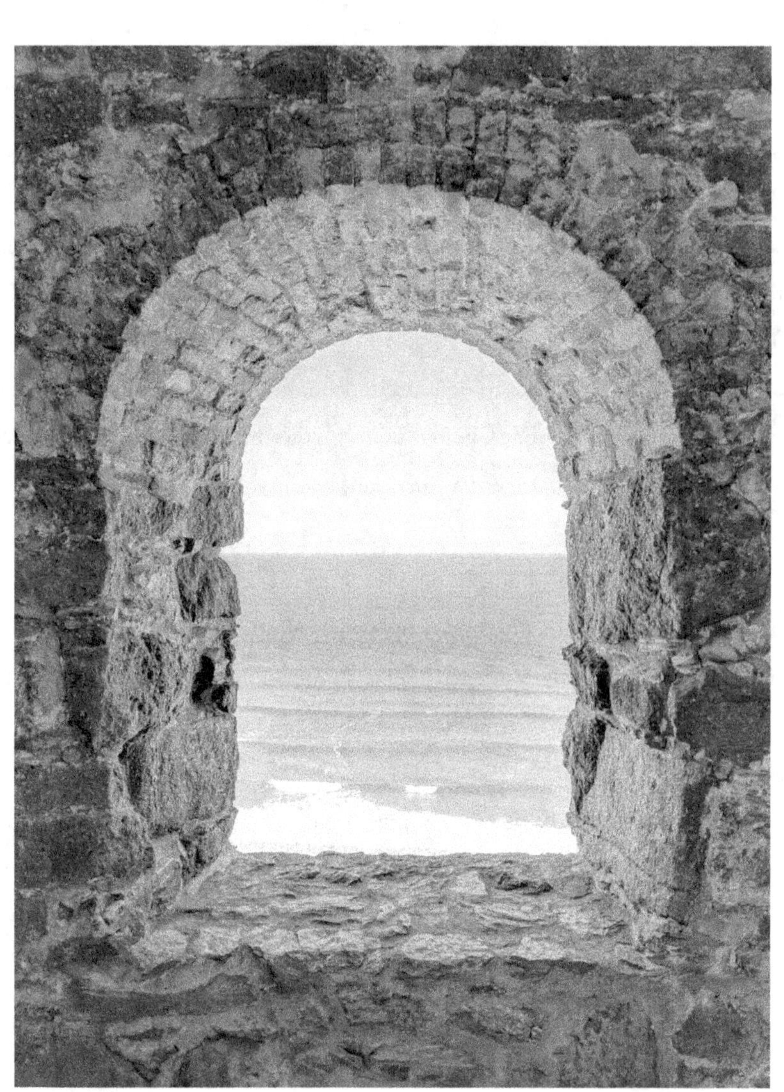

"But I am afraid

to

bare my soul

to

a god

I do not know."

This is a verse from the first poem I wrote, called "Afraid."
The poem was written three months before I prayed and gave my heart to God.

~~~~~~~~~~~~~~~~~~~~

"In the beginning God created the heavens and the earth. Now the earth was formless and empty, darkness was over the surface of the deep, and the spirit of God was hovering over the waters."
(Genesis 1:1–2, NIV)

These are the first words in the Old Testament written by Moses.

~~~~~~~~~~~~~~~~~~~~

"In the beginning was the Word, and the Word was with God, and the Word was God. He was with God in the beginning. Through him all things were made; without him nothing was made that has been made. In him was life, and that life was the light of all mankind. The light shines in the darkness, and the darkness has not overcome it." (John 1:1–5, NIV)

These are the first words in the Gospel according to John.

Thank You, God.

TABLE OF CONTENTS

Introduction — 2

Afraid—*Poem* — A poem about the admiration a non-believer in Christ Jesus has for a believer. — 7

Testimony — My testimony about my return to God after leaving Him 50 years earlier. — 17

Never Let Go—*Poem* — A poem about our unconditional love for people close to us and God's unconditional love for all. — 27

Spiritual Renewal—*Inspiration* — This inspiration came to me when God put me in a situation to talk with a homeless man. — 37

Finding Home—*Poem* — A poem about where our true home is. God's love for us and our love of God is our eternal home. — 47

Surrender—*Poem* — Surrendering our life to God requires us to change our hearts. — 57

Todd's Prayer—*Inspiration* — Stop and see what God wants you to see; stop and listen to what God wants you to hear. — 69

I Don't Know—*Inspiration* — Sometimes we do not know what God is trying to tell us or where He is leading us. — 81

Dear God—*Poem* — A poem about questioning our faith. When we question our faith, we are questioning God's plan. God has given us the ability to choose; choose wisely. — 95

My Heart Aches—*Poem* — God wants us to be disciples of His Word, but this can be difficult and sometimes the timing is not right to preach the Word of God to others. — 105

I Try To Live Like Jesus—*Poem* — Every day we need to work hard to live like Jesus. Doing so brings us more peace. — 115

Don't Cry—*Poem* — We are sinners. We are not perfect. We are flawed. Do not be afraid to expose your handicaps to God. — 125

Broken—*Poem* — We are all broken. Trust God and pray for those who are lost and do not know God. God will heal broken souls. — 137

Grace—*Inspiration* — When we sin, we ask God for forgiveness. Through God's grace, our sins are forgiven. We also need to forgive ourselves and give ourselves the same grace we receive from God. — 149

I AM Part I—*Poem* — The first four "I Am" verses which occur in the Book of John in chapters 6–10. — 159

I AM Part II—*Poem* — The final three "I Am" verses and a poem referencing Exodus 3:14 when God said to Moses, "I AM WHO I AM. This is what you are to say to the Israelites: 'I AM has sent me to you.'" — 177

The Blessing — 193

Appendix — 199

Conversation—*Poem* — 201

Conversation 2022—*Poem* — 205

About the Author — 213

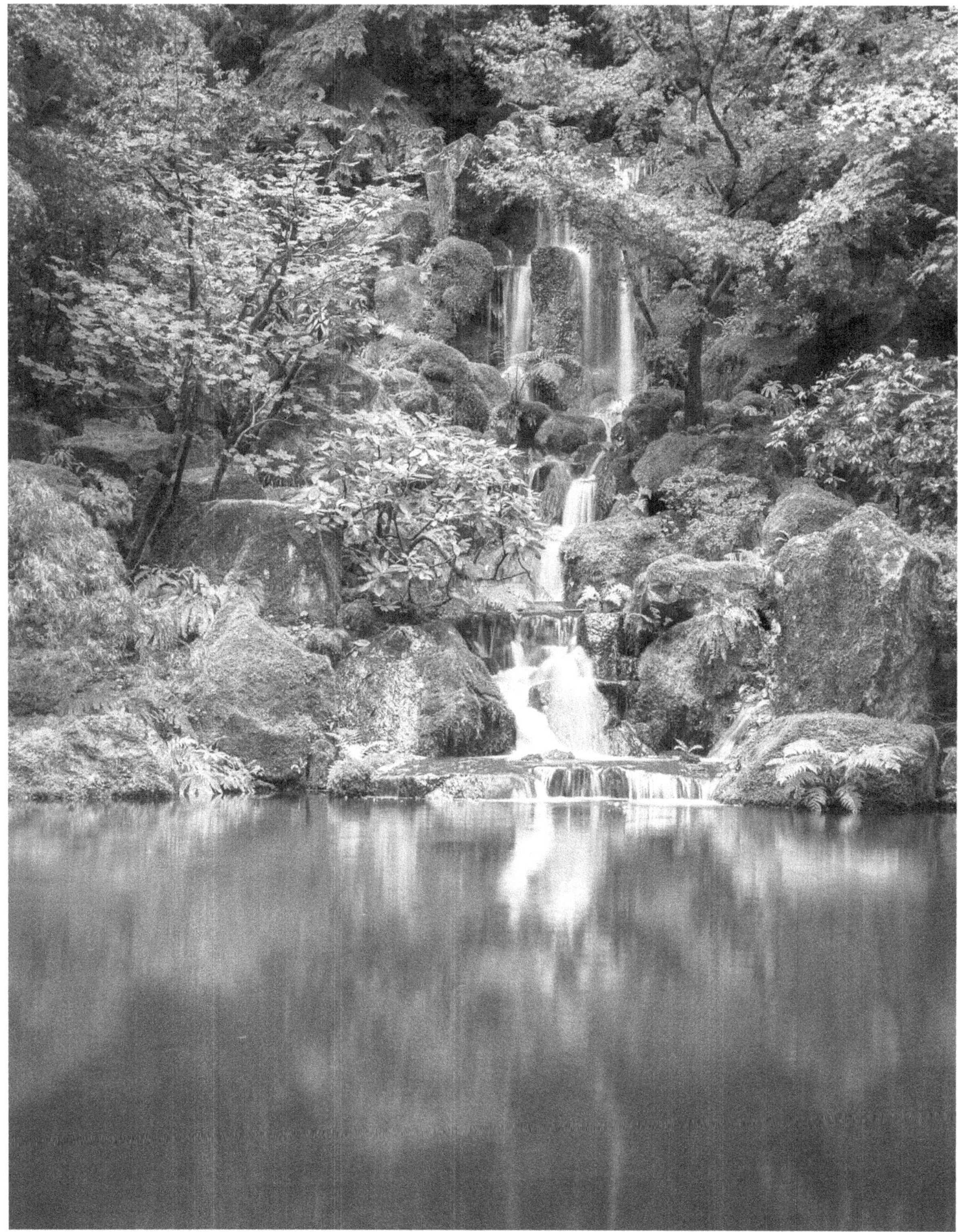

Acknowledgments

IN THE BEGINNING of our own lives, from the moment we take our first breath outside of the womb, we are influenced every day by hundreds or thousands of things—sights, sounds, light, darkness, noise, people, birds, the sun, and so on and so on. The poems and inspirational writings in this book are all a reflection of these kinds of influences on my life and experiences that have been provided to me by God.

I would first like to thank God my Father. Everything I have I owe to God. Thank you, God, for being my Father and providing me with what I have; thank You for leading me down the paths You have, and thank you for encouraging me to write these poems and inspirations.

The second thank you is to myself. I like to say, we need to love God, then we need to love ourselves, and then we are able to love others. One of my inspirational writings in this book, titled "Grace," is about how we are too hard on ourselves, and we need to give ourselves more grace. We need to give ourselves grace the same way God gives us grace. By thanking myself, I am saying that I am proud of myself for coming back to God after a fifty-year absence. (You will read more about this in my testimony.) And I am also thanking myself for taking the time to write this book and listening to God, who inspired me.

Everything I have written has a very deep meaning for me. Many of the writings were influenced by something I saw, a story I was told, or a situation I was in. For example, the poem "Broken" was written after I saw a half-naked homeless woman on the street, dancing erratically, very high on drugs. To this day I still have a vision of that woman. It was God who brought me to that street corner to see that poor, broken woman. And it was God who inspired me to write about her.

Third, I would like to thank my family, and especially my wife Cathy. She is a rock. She too left God for many years. Although she was not a practicing Christian for many years, she still led her life with Christian values. In the Appendix of this book, there are two poems about our life together, written thirty-nine years apart. The first poem was my wedding vow to her in 1983, called "Conversation," and the second one is a follow up to "Conversation," written for our thirty-ninth wedding anniversary. It is called "Conversation 2022." If Cathy were not in my life, I am not sure if I would have come back to God and been born again. Thank you, Cathy, for loving me through the ups and downs.

I would also like to thank my parents for raising me with strong values and for teaching me the difference between right and wrong.

I would like to thank Nick Herb. When I was a young adult, Nick encouraged me to come back to God.

I would like to thank my stepmother, Lauren Fenz, for praying for me and I would also like to thank her for bringing my father back to God.

I would also like to thank Pastor Ivory Crittendon for trying to lead me back to our Lord. I believe God put all these people in my life to guide me down the path back to Him.

A special thank you also goes to my editor, Arlyn Lawrence, founder of Inspira Literary Solutions. This book would not have been published without the expertise of Arlyn and her team.

Finally, I would like to thank Kira Crandall. Kira is a young woman who lived with my wife and I for a few months. She is a strong Christian and would read the Bible every morning. More than once, she would say, "Brien, you should pray and give your heart to God," and I would say, "No, I am fine." Then one day, when she said, "Brien, you should pray and give your heart to God", I said "YES"—and my life changed FOREVER.

FOREVER IS A REALLY LONG TIME.

Thank You, God, for sending all these people to me.

INTRODUCTION

In the beginning ...

God should be our inspiration for everything. I have written this book with inspirations I have received from God. If we put ourselves in God's world—His Kingdom—and by this, I mean we pray, we worship, and we live our lives for God and according to God's Way—God will bring us into inspirational moments. Inspirational moments are unique for each of us, and learning to recognize them is one of the steps we take in building our personal relationship with God.

I believe I was inspired by God to write this book. I wrote it for Him, and I trust that He will guide me in its distribution. A friend recently told me that he believes God inspires people He knows will work hard for Him, and gives them the strength to do it. Although there was a lot of work that went into writing the book, it never felt like work. This book is a collection of eighteen different poems and inspirational writings; each one is a chapter. The chapters are organized in chronological order as to when God inspired me. Some of the poems or inspirations were written at the time I was inspired, and others were written later, but the order in the book is chronological.

I recommend you read a chapter a day as a daily devotion. There are four or five sections to each chapter. Reading through a chapter and listening to the recommended worship music takes approximately fifteen minutes.

The first page for the chapters that are "poems" are stories explaining the inspiration I received from God to write that poem. For the chapters that are "inspirations," the writing itself is the explanation. After each poem or inspiration, I have referenced scripture that is meaningful to the poem or inspirational writing. Following the scripture is a prayer. Each prayer relates to the personal meaning I received from the poem or inspiration. I have also included some reflection questions to guide your own thoughts and prayers.

I close each chapter with worship music recommendations. I hope you take the time to listen and or watch one or two of the songs. Each recommended song is an important part of the message of each chapter. I enjoy watching the worship music on YouTube; just search for the songs using the search bar. You may also choose to use Spotify or Pandora or iTunes, or any other music app, but I like YouTube because I find that watching the artists perform the songs is as powerful as the songs themselves. There are many versions of a song on YouTube. Find a version that is the most meaningful to you. You can also bring a song up on your cell phone by scanning the QR code provided for each song.

I hope as you read each chapter that you feel some of the same inspiration I felt when God inspired me to write. And I hope it helps you further build and grow your personal relationship with Him, our Father. If you have not prayed and given your heart to God, I hope this book inspires you too not be "afraid." The first poem in the book is titled "Afraid" and there is a verse in the poem:

"But I am afraid to bare my soul to a God I do not know."

If you do not know God, do not be afraid to bare your soul. If you do know God, bare your soul to Him even more.

God loves you.

DAILY PRAYER

"Lord, my sins are ever with me.

I deserve Your judgment.

Thank You for the great mercy

I have received through

Jesus's death for me.

That He died in my place must

always be the primary

reality in my life."[1]

---

1 Footnote reference from Micah 7:18–20 in the *NIV Study Bible.*

AFRAID

AFRAID

A Poem

THE POEM "AFRAID" was the first poem I had written in over forty years, in August of 2019. And it is the first poem I wrote about my spiritual journey. It was written three months before I prayed and renewed my faith in God. In inspiring me to write this poem, God knew I would be coming back to Him soon. I see this poem as one of the steps God was having me take before I become a born-again Christian. God was leading me down a path that would change my life forever.

It was written from the perspective of someone admiring the "faith" that another person has in God but being "afraid" to commit to that "faith." They have deep reverence for the love and kindness of the Word and the eternal life it brings, but they are afraid. And, as a line from the poem says,

"But I am afraid to bare my soul to a God I do not know."

The first person I shared the poem with was a young woman who was living with my wife and me. A couple of months after I wrote the poem, she invited me to pray and give my heart to God and I said yes. I could never have imagined how saying "yes" would forever change my life. God was using her as the final person in my life to bring me back to God. There were others before her, equally as important, who also tried to guide me back to the Lord. After being born again, I found out from my stepmother that she and my father had prayed for me. I am sure there were others praying too.

The Lord truly works miracles.

God,
Thank You for sending people to pray for me.

AFRAID

You have love and grace and kindness
You have faith in God the one
You know that life's eternal
And love will overcome

I'm afraid to show a true belief
Afraid to show my heart
I'm hoping I can see the light
And come in from the dark

Afraid, afraid to open up my heart
Afraid, afraid, not knowing where to start
Afraid to say, I need some help, and afraid to look above
Afraid to open up my life to God's eternal love

Your path is guided by His love
Your days are guided so
You have felt His love eternal
He has touched your damaged soul

I see no reason, why I should change, I know my life is hollow
I do not know of what you say … is this the road to follow
I do not have the faith you do, that guides your every day
I reach and hope to see the light, but clouds are in my way

Afraid, afraid to open up my heart

Afraid, afraid, not knowing where to start

Afraid to say, I need some help, and afraid to look above

Afraid to open up my life to God's eternal love

You know that life's eternal, if we give our heart to Him

You know that He will guide our path even as we sin

You know that healing takes His love and our love in return

And at the time of judgment, eternal life's confirmed

But I am afraid to bare my soul, to a God I do not know

You ask me why? … And all I say, I know not where to go

Is it fear of what can't be seen or fear because I sin?

Or is it fear, because I know, eternal life's with Him?

Afraid, afraid to open up my heart

Afraid, afraid, not knowing where to start

Afraid to say, I need some help, and afraid to look above

Afraid to open up my life to God's eternal love

Mark 4:13–20, NIV

Then Jesus said the them, "Don't you understand this parable? How then will you understand any parable? The farmer sows the word. Some people are like seed along the path, where the word is sown. As soon as they hear it, Satan comes and takes away the word that was sown in them.

"Others, like seed sown on rocky places, hear the word and at once receive it with joy. But since they have no root, they last only a short time.When trouble or persecution comes because of the word, they quickly fall away.

"Still others, like seed sown among thorns, hear the word; but the worries of this life, the deceitfulness of wealth and the desires for other things come in and choke the word, making it unfruitful. Others, like seed sown on good soil, hear the word, accept it, and produce a crop ... some thirty, some a hundred times what was sown."

My Prayer for Those Who Are Afraid

Dear God,

At some point we were all afraid. Thank You for making me not afraid. Thank You for guiding me back to You. Thank You for bringing all the people into my life that helped guide me back to you.

Please God, help the people who are still afraid. Help them bare their souls to a God that they will soon know. Help them know the love and the peace you bring to our lives. Give them the strength to reach out to You and know that if they pray and make You the Lord of their lives, that their sins will be forgiven, and they will receive eternal life with You.

"My Lord and my God!" (John 21:28, NIV)

Your loving and devoted son,
Amen

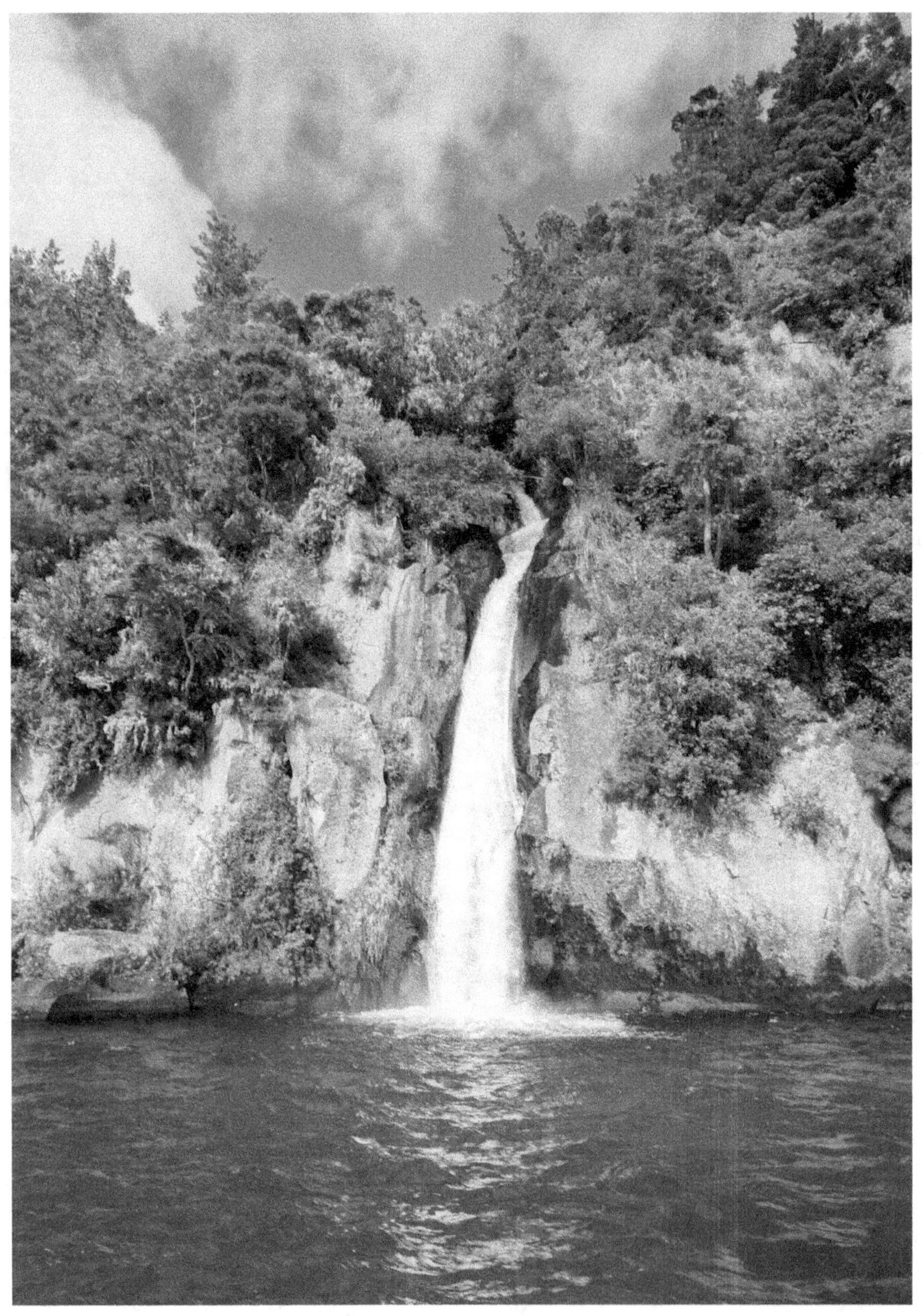

Reflections for Your Journey

1. What can you do to *"open up your life to God's eternal love"*?

2. Think of a time when God brought someone into your life to guide you to (or back to) Him. How did that person's influence affect or inspire you?

3. How has God *"touched your damaged soul"*?

4. Has something ever happened to you that you felt was a miracle? What message do you think God was sending you?

WORSHIP MUSIC RECOMMENDATIONS

Oceans (Where Feet May Fail) • Hillsong UNITED, Taya Smith
youtube.com/watch?v=OP-00EwLdiU 

 *The Blood* • Bethel Music with Jenn Johnson & Mitch Wong
youtube.com/watch?v=4DtiMf1xoLM

TESTIMONY

TESTIMONY

I WAS BORN IN 1957, and my father's family was a religious one; his parents, along with their family, would attend church every Sunday. My father and his brother and sister all attended Christian schools at some point in their education. When my parents married, our family also attended church every Sunday and after church the kids would go to Sunday School. I have two sisters and all three of us were baptized, and celebrated our first communions and confirmations at our church.

When I was about thirteen or fourteen, my dad stopped going to church. I do not know why, but for a teenage boy, not having to attend church every Sunday and Sunday School was truly "a gift from God." When my dad left God, I left God too and did not return for fifty years.

During those years, I attended church infrequently and, in many ways, led an ungodly life. In my mid-thirties, I started thinking about coming back to God, but I did not know how. Christian friends would invite me to Christian events, but I was not inspired to come back to our Lord. At these events I felt like an outsider even though they had something I wanted.

A few years ago, my wife and I took a young woman into our home. She was between jobs, and we felt we could provide her with some guidance. We were empty nesters and had an extra bedroom in our home. (I mentioned her in my Acknowledgments, when I was thanking God, and all the people God brought to me.)

She is a musician and, one day, after a late-night performance, she slept at the studio where she records. She called me and asked if I could bring her something from home. I went to the studio to bring her what she needed, and we started talking about her life and how she was doing. During that conversation she said, "Brien, you should pray and give your heart to God." She had asked me this before, but this time I said,

"YES…I will give my heart to God!"

Those words changed my life forever. Those words have made me a better man. Those words have made me a better husband. Those words have made me a better father. Those words brought me back to God my Father, whom I had left fifty years prior.

Truthfully, my first thought when I said, "Yes, I will give my heart to God," was, *What have I done?* I feared the unknown. I didn't know God.

How would I get to know God? I knew I needed to be sincere about getting to know Him, but I did not know where to start.

Shortly after we prayed, our young friend said, "we need to go to the Christian bookstore and buy you a Bible." At that moment, I went from being afraid to being really afraid. Reflecting back, even though I was afraid, I kept saying "YES" to whatever she asked me to do. I also felt I had made a promise to God and down deep I did not want to break that promise. I truly believe that God knew this was my time to come home.

We left the studio that day and went to a Christian bookstore to buy my NIV Study Bible. She told me I should start by reading the Book of John in the New Testament. I went home and tried to read the Book of John, but I did not understand the chapter and verse layout. And because this Bible is a study Bible, I was confused with the NIV footnotes and study comments. I put the Bible on my shelf and did not open it for over a month. I also did not tell my wife that I had prayed and given my heart to God.

A few weeks later, feeling anxious because I had not moved forward, I told my wife what I had done and that I wanted God in my life and in our marriage. We had a wonderful conversation about our child-hoods as Catholics and that we both had missed God for many years. A couple of weeks later, we went to church with the young woman who was living with us and, since then, we have both been growing our personal relationships with God.

I gave my heart to God in October of 2019. The first poem in this book is "Afraid." It was written in August of 2019, three months before I prayed and gave my heart to God. Every time I read "Afraid," I realize that God knew I was coming back to Him, and I also realize that I am afraid no longer.

"Do not be afraid; God loves you."

If you declare with your mouth, "Jesus is Lord," and believe in your heart that God raised him from the dead, you will be saved. For it is with your heart that you believe and are justified, and it is with your mouth that you profess your faith and are saved. As Scripture says, "Anyone who believes in him will never be put to shame."

My Prayer for Those Who Have Given Their Heart to God

Dear God,

Thank You for leading me and all who have prayed to You to guide us. We thank You for everything You have provided for us. You are our Father and we are Your children. As Song of Solomon 6:3 says, "I am my beloved's and he is mine" (NIV). Our lives are forever changed when we pray and say, "YES … I will give my heart to God."

Each one of us has our own personal testimony. Each one of us has our own story about praying and coming to You. This "new beginning" is also the time where each one of us starts to build our personal relationship with You. God, please guide us and let us know what we can do as Your disciples to help others pray and give their hearts to You.

"My Lord and my God!" (John 21:28, NIV)

Your loving and devoted son,
Amen

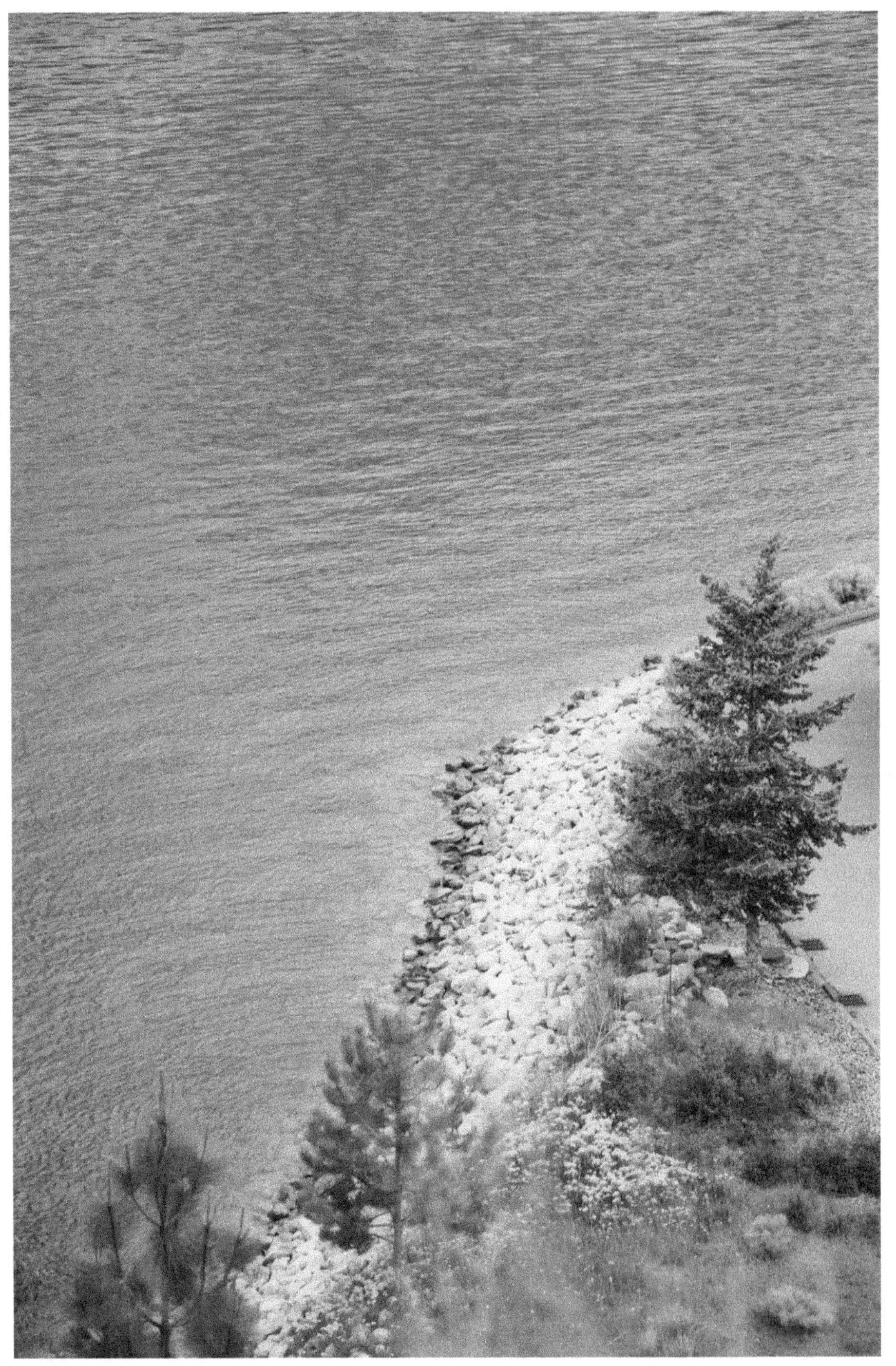

Reflections for Your Journey

1. If you have a personal relationship with Jesus already, reflect on your life before and after you made Him your Lord and Savior. How has life changed? If you left our Lord for a period, reflect on why this occurred.

2. Reflect on the individuals who helped you make Jesus Christ your Lord and Savior. How can you be an encouragement to others the way these individuals were to you?

3. There are inevitably times when we question our faith. What is one thing you can do every day to keep your faith strong?

4. If you have not yet made Jesus Christ your Lord and Savior, what questions do you have and whom could you talk with to address these questions?

WORSHIP MUSIC RECOMMENDATIONS

Say I Won't • MercyMe
youtube.com/watch?v=UhTHgaCjTJs 

 *Left It in the Water* • We the Kingdom
youtube.com/watch?v=g2RuFXttmxk

I Can Only Imagine (Movie Sound Track) • MercyMe 
youtube.com/watch?v=-CIXaoRyseU

NEVER LET GO

Never Let Go

A Poem

THE SECOND SPIRITUAL POEM I WROTE, "Never Let Go," is about how believing in "The Word" changes how you view and feel about relationships with others. God's Word provides hope and love.

The poem was written as a gift from me to the young woman who was living with my wife and me. She was the one who asked me to pray and give my heart to God. I wanted to give her something that would show her how much she means to me. She struggles with insecurities, as we all do. It is God's love and warmth that comforts us and gives us peace.

So many of the Scriptures are about love. We first need to love God, then love ourselves, and then love our family and friends. Loving others and showing our love for them is very important to our own spiritual journey.

Love is about kindness and appreciating others. We can never tell anyone too many times that we love them. We need to try and not be uncomfortable telling someone we love them. And, most importantly, every day we need to tell God how much we love Him and appreciate the grace He gives us. As a line in the poem says, "God said, 'Believe, have Faith, and Love will show…'"

God has true and unconditional love for us. Pray to God and let Him know you love Him. Send these words as a gift of love to someone you love.

"Love you so; never let go."

God,

Love You so; never let go.

NEVER LET GO

God brought us a child, broken and hurt
He said, "Take care of her
She is a beautiful child"
Love her so; never let go

She's seen God's light
But did not know
I told myself…
Love you so; never let go

She asked, "If God's light is love, where is this love?
What is this spirit and almighty from above?"
She is lost, so lost, and did not know
Love you so; never let go

She has pain and fear and a broken heart
She is afraid to trust and confused to start
God said, "Believe in Me; have faith and love will show"
Love you so; never let go

She opened up and looked above
A miracle occurred
It was God's love
Love you so; never let go

God brought her love

From where she did not know

"Why would they help, I am wounded so"

Love you so; never let go

The strangers' love drew deep and wide

It was supportive with no divide

Unconditional with no hurt

Love you so; never let go

True Love was what she felt

Was this God's plan; was this her path to take

Or just another road at stake

Love you so; never let go

From True Love she found her own

They touched, they kissed, a spark was born

God's love and theirs, was the cure

Love you so, Never let go

Her heart opened to let God in

This was her path … God, her Lord, and Him

She now has love and spiritual light

Love you so; never let go

BEAUTIFUL CHILD,

WE LOVE YOU SO AND WILL NEVER LET GO

Psalm 139:17–18, NIV

How precious to me are your thoughts, God!

How vast is the sum of them!

Were I to count them,

they would outnumber the grains of sand—

when I am awake, I am still with you.

My Prayer about God's Eternal Love

Dear God,

Your unconditional and eternal love for us is amazing. As we build our relationship with You, the power of this love becomes even stronger. As we build our relationship with You, we understand more and more that this love is truly unconditional and forever. We are Your children, and You are our Father. And we are here to serve Your Word and serve You. We know we are sinners, but we try hard not to sin. The power of Your love is so strong that when we do sin, and we confess our sins, You will forgive us. What is important is that we continue to have faith and every day try hard to further build our faith in You. We know that it is our faith that will give us eternal life in Heaven.

"My Lord and my God!" John 21:28, NIV

Your loving and devoted son,
Amen

Reflections for Your Journey

1. Find a scripture that expresses hope and love and write it down here or somewhere you can see it and be encouraged by it.

2. What gift of unconditional love could you give to someone special in your life?

3. Psalm 139:17–18 says that God's precious thoughts outnumber the grains of sand. How do God's precious thoughts affect you every day?

4. Think of a time in your life, or the life of someone you know, when God's unconditional love helped you (or them) heal.

WORSHIP MUSIC RECOMMENDATIONS

Reckless Love • Cory Ashbury, from the Rutherford County Prison 
youtube.com/watch?v=aZyvhtvNO4I

 *You Say* • Lauren Daigle
youtube.com/watch?v=sIaT8Jl2zpI

SPIRITUAL RENEWAL

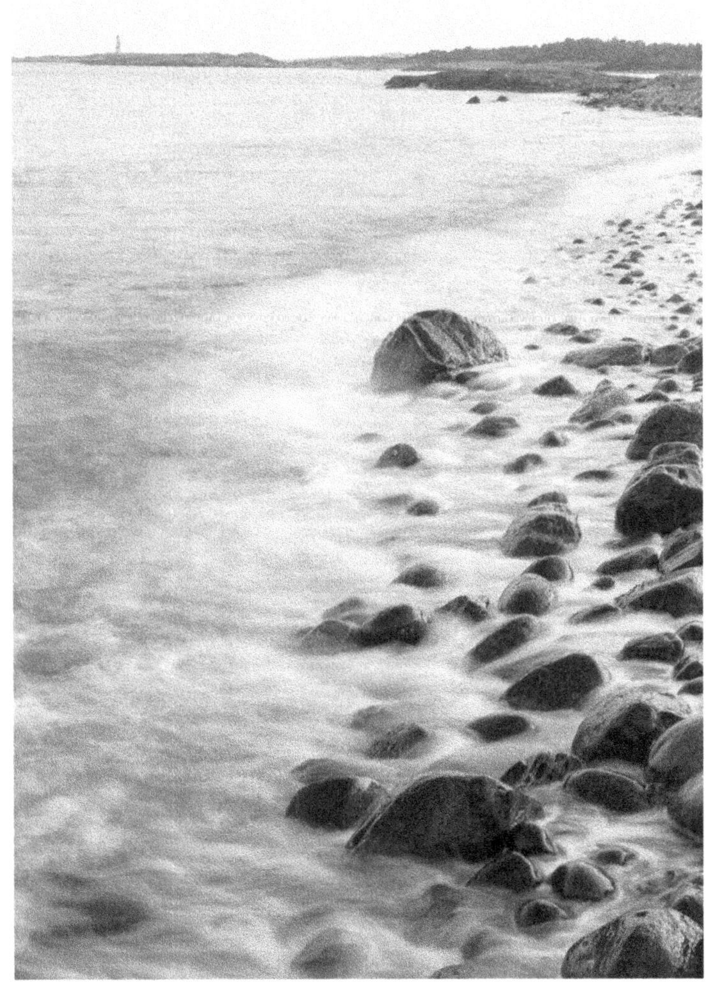

SPIRITUAL RENEWAL

An Inspiration

IN JANUARY OF 2020, just a couple of months after I became a "born-again Christian," I was driving my mom to Palm Springs. We had been on the road for a couple of hours and pulled into a freeway rest stop. Walking to the men's room, I saw a homeless young man sitting on the sidewalk. I avoided eye contact and went on my way.

When I was walking back to the car, I had a feeling that I should stop and engage in a brief conversation with him. I kneeled and said, "Excuse me, are you okay?"

He replied, "I am fine. I am just going through a rough spot."

I asked him, "Do you have any family?"

He said he had a wife and a child in Chehalis.

I asked him, "Is it drugs?"

He said, "No, it wasn't drugs. I am just going through a rough spot."

I said to him, "Have you thought about God?"

He said, "I have a Bible at home."

I told him that God loves him.

And he said, "I know he does."

I wished him well and went back to my car.

"Spiritual renewal begins with putting an end to one's unjust treatment of others.

This is not all there is, but it is an essential first step."

NIV Study Bible

This quote is from the introduction section of the Book of Micah in my NIV Study Bible. It summarizes my experience with the young man. Being "born again" provides us with a path to open our hearts and let the Holy Spirit come in. Living "in" the Holy Spirit allows us to have a spiritual renewal.

My very brief conversation with this young man had a profound impact on me. Over the next few days, I reflected on it many times. Why did I reflect on this encounter? I truly believe that God wanted me to engage with him. I truly believe that God was sending me a message. And I truly believe that God felt, at this point in my spiritual journey, that I was ready to understand God's message of love. I had become a Christian only three months before this encounter. And I believe the message that God was sending me was that this young man is my brother, and he is loved by God in the same way that God loves all of us.

God wanted me to understand that I, too, need to love this hurt and confused young man, just as I love my family and friends. We are all children of God and so much of God's message is about love. Since that day, I have tried very hard to look at people who are hurt and confused with the compassion and love that God wants us to have. We need to pray for all who are hurt and confused.

I truly believe that when I was returning to my car from the restroom that it was God who inspired me to stop and talk with this young man. God knew it was time for me to move to the next level in understanding His Word—and this was my opportunity.

A few weeks later, I was telling this story to a member of our church. In telling the story, I became very emotional. This too was another step forward for me in understanding God's Word and understanding what God wants from and for all His children.

I have often wondered what happened to that young man. Where is he? Is he safe? Was he able to get help? I hope so. My encounter with him was very powerful. I wish I could tell him the story I just told you. I would like to thank him for talking with me. I told my pastor this story and he said, "Maybe the young man was an angel sent from God." Maybe?

God, please look closely over that young man and, if possible, let him know that he is a very important part of my spiritual renewal and journey. Also, please let him know that I love him.

God,
Watch over that young man and help him find peace.

Luke 14:11, NIV

"For all those who exalt themselves will be humbled,

and those who humble themselves will be exalted."

John 14:27, NIV

"Peace I leave with you; my peace I give you. I do not give as the world gives.

Do not let your hearts be troubled and do not be afraid."

My Prayer for Those Who Are Seeking Peace and Spiritual Renewal

Dear God,

When I first came to You, I felt peace. This peace comes from knowing that You are with us, You love us, and You will not go away. As the Book of John says in Chapter 14, verse 27, "Peace I leave with you; my peace I give you." I have tried to explain this feeling of peace and warmth to others. Sometimes it is difficult for others to understand the feeling of peace. Please bring to those who are seeking to know You the same feeling of peace that you brought me. It is from this feeling of peace that we learn of Your eternal love and then learn to love others as You command us. For all those who are seeking peace and spiritual renewal, I say, "Peace be with you."

"My Lord and my God!" John 21:28, NIV

Your loving and devoted son,

Amen

Reflections for Your Journey

1. How does God humble you?

2. Describe a time that you were more focused on exalting yourself than God, and were humbled. (See Luke 14:11 to learn what God thinks about this.)

3. Reflect on a time you have felt a sense of warmth and peace from God.

4. What can you change or implement in your life so you can better feel the warmth and peace that God brings?

WORSHIP MUSIC RECOMMENDATIONS

Greater Still • Brandon Lake
youtube.com/watch?v=-0Zrn1o0VXY 

 *Look What You've Done* • Tasha Layton
youtube.com/watch?v=cBw1ZmBi7ZI

FINDING HOME

FINDING HOME

A Poem

THE THIRD SPIRITUAL POEM I wrote is called "Finding Home." I was inspired to write this poem based on two very powerful and moving experiences. The first occurred while I was on vacation in Cabo San Lucas with my wife in October of 2020. It had been almost a year since I'd prayed and made God the Lord of my life. My wife and I were both enjoying feeling more fulfilled and committed to each other, having brought God into our lives.

Late one afternoon, sitting around the pool, I felt for the first time in my life that I was truly "home." Faith in God had given me a spiritual peace that I had never felt before. I felt at home with God and my wife. I was right where I was supposed to be. I was right where God wanted me to be.

The second inspiration for this poem came a couple of weeks later when I was ministering with three Christian men at a homeless encampment in Tacoma, Washington. It was the first time I had been in a homeless encampment, and it was a very eye-opening experience. After walking into the encampment, I quickly realized that I was in the "home" of the homeless. This is where they lived, and their home required from me the same respect that I would expect from them if they were in my home. I needed to ignore the filth, the garbage, and the smell. I also realized that home is just a place. Our eternal "home" is with God our Father.

When I was ministering to a young woman in the homeless encampment, whom I assumed was high on drugs, suddenly she started to recite the Lord's Prayer. My first thought was, *In her past she had God in her life. I wonder what tragedies and emotional trauma brought her to where she is today?*

The Dutch Catholic priest and author, Henri Nouwen, once said,
"True community is the place where the individual we least like
always lives next door."

God,

Please bless that young woman and all like her who are lost. I pray for her safety and hopefully a return to You and a life away from homelessness and drugs.

FINDING HOME

I walk a mile the road less known
A journey's drift I had no home
I looked above at scatter clouds
My soul was lost; it shouted loud

Was home a place of sheltered wealth
Or a place where souls reached out for help
Was home a place of physical touch
Or a place where souls are sheltered much

Was home a place where spirits spoke
Or a place where souls found all hope
A place of light and peace and love
A place we thought may be above

Was home a place with a distance past
A place with prophets and a God to last
Could I touch this home or do I just believe
Is home the place where love's received

I came to believe that home is Him
That His love of me makes home begin
He brings me peace and I bring faith
And with His love, partners we make

It takes faith to be God's shelter kin
It takes faith to know your home's with Him
It takes faith to know and truly see
That our home's with God for eternity

Mark 12:28–31, NIV

One of the teachers of the law came and heard them debating.

Noticing that Jesus had given them a good answer,

he asked them, "Of all the commandments, which one is the most important?"

"The most important one," answered Jesus, "is this: 'Hear, O Israel: The Lord our God, the Lord is one.

Love the Lord your God with all your heart and with all your soul and with all your mind and with all your

strength. The second is this: 'Love your neighbor as yourself.' There is no command greater than these.'"

My Prayer for Those Who Are Lost and Have Not Found Home

Dear God,

Finding You and understanding the love You have forY our children has brought peace to my life. I would like to pray for those who are seeking peace. I would like to pray for those who know nothing of Your peace. Please give them the strength to continue to reach out and find You. Please give them the strength to not give up. Please give them the strength to feel the love You give. And please give them the strength to find Home. It is Your love that truly is our Home.

God, so many people are lost today. Please help them because helping them helps us all. I would also like to pray for the young woman I met in the homeless encampment three years ago. I hope she is safe. You know where she is. Please keep her safe. She is an important person in my spiritual journey. She helped me realize that finding You is "finding Home."

"My Lord and my God!" John 21:28, NIV

Your loving and devoted son,
Amen

1. Do you place a higher value on your home and personal possessions than you do on your relationship with God? How does this play out in your life?

2. Does it raise to the level of idolatry? Why or why not?

3. How have you handled a time when you had to either live with or live close to someone you least liked?

4. How would you handle this situation today?

WORSHIP MUSIC RECOMMENDATIONS

 *Finally Home* • MercyMe
youtube.com/watch?v=HNIHuKTunDA

In The Room • Matt Maher 
youtube.com/watch?v=sF-Uw5MwZg0

 *Thank God I Do* • Lauren Daigle
youtube.com/watch?v=OoEr8BSsrxg

SURRENDER

SURRENDER

A Poem

THE FOURTH POEM I wrote after coming home to God is called "Surrender." I was driving to a client meeting from Tacoma to Packwood, Washington, which is about a two-hour drive. I started thinking about how bringing God into our lives requires us to bring Him deep into our hearts, and requires us also to *change* our hearts. Everything needs to change. As lines in the poem say,

> *Change of love to find our way*
> *Change of life in every day*
> *Change of heart … surrender*

God has given us free will. We have the freedom to choose. Adam and Eve had the freedom to choose but, unfortunately, they chose wrong. God does not want to control our actions, but He does want us, through our faith in Him, to make choices that would please Him. I once heard in a sermon that a sin is anything that would not please God.

Fully surrendering our hearts to God is very hard. God gave us the freedom to choose but too often we feel our way is the correct way, even though it may conflict with God's will. We cannot see God, but we feel God's presence through the Holy Spirit and our faith. God's way is the only way.

One way I've learned to surrender to God is through a *novena* prayer, a Catholic devotional practice that lasts for nine days. The tradition of praying a *novena* (which comes from the root word for "nine") memorializes the nine days following His ascension into Heaven that Jesus' followers spent "…joined together constantly in prayer, along with the women and Mary the mother of Jesus, and with his brothers" (Acts 1:14).

They remained there together until Pentecost, when the Holy Spirit came, filling them with grace, courage, and power—so much so that that very day 3,000 more people came to faith in Christ! This has served as a model for the novena. You bring your trials and struggles to God, seek daily Him with all your heart, and wait for the Holy Spirit, responding to His answer with praise and thankfulness.

Father Don Dolindo (1882–1979) received from Jesus the word of the "Surrender Novena." Each day of the Surrender Novena is a different prayer, with the last line in prayer being, "O Jesus, I surrender myself to you, take of everything." This line is then recited ten times:

Day 1 of the Surrender Novena
"Why do you confuse yourself by worrying? Leave the care of your affairs to Me and everything will be peaceful. I say to you in truth that every act of true, blind, complete surrender to Me produces the effect that you desire and resolves all difficult situations."
"O Jesus, I surrender myself to you, take of everything." (This line is recited ten times.)

Perhaps you may find this practice helpful. But whether you do or not, surrendering to God is getting down on our knees, lifting our arms high in the air, looking up, and saying, **"God, I have faith. I surrender my heart to You. You are my Father, and I am Your child. Your will is my will. I am here to follow Your Word and help bring others to You."**

God,

Please help me to always have faith, to never question my faith, and to never question Your way.
With all my love, with my arms reached high, fully surrendering my heart to Your will,

Your servant in love,
Amen

SURRENDER

Change of heart when God's let in
Change of souls that are too thin
Change of why we're here today
Change of heart ... surrender

Change of love to find our way
Change of life in every day
Change of life in shape and form
Change of heart ... surrender

Change of how we hear and see
Change of how we look at thee
Change in how we view our past
Change of heart ... surrender

Change in what we know will come
Change of how we pray for one
Change of what the future brings
Change of heart... surrender

Change in knowing where we'll go
Change in how we know we know
Change in how we feel your love
Change of heart ... surrender

Change of heart when God's let in
Change in grace as we sin
Change we feel forevermore
Change of heart ... surrender

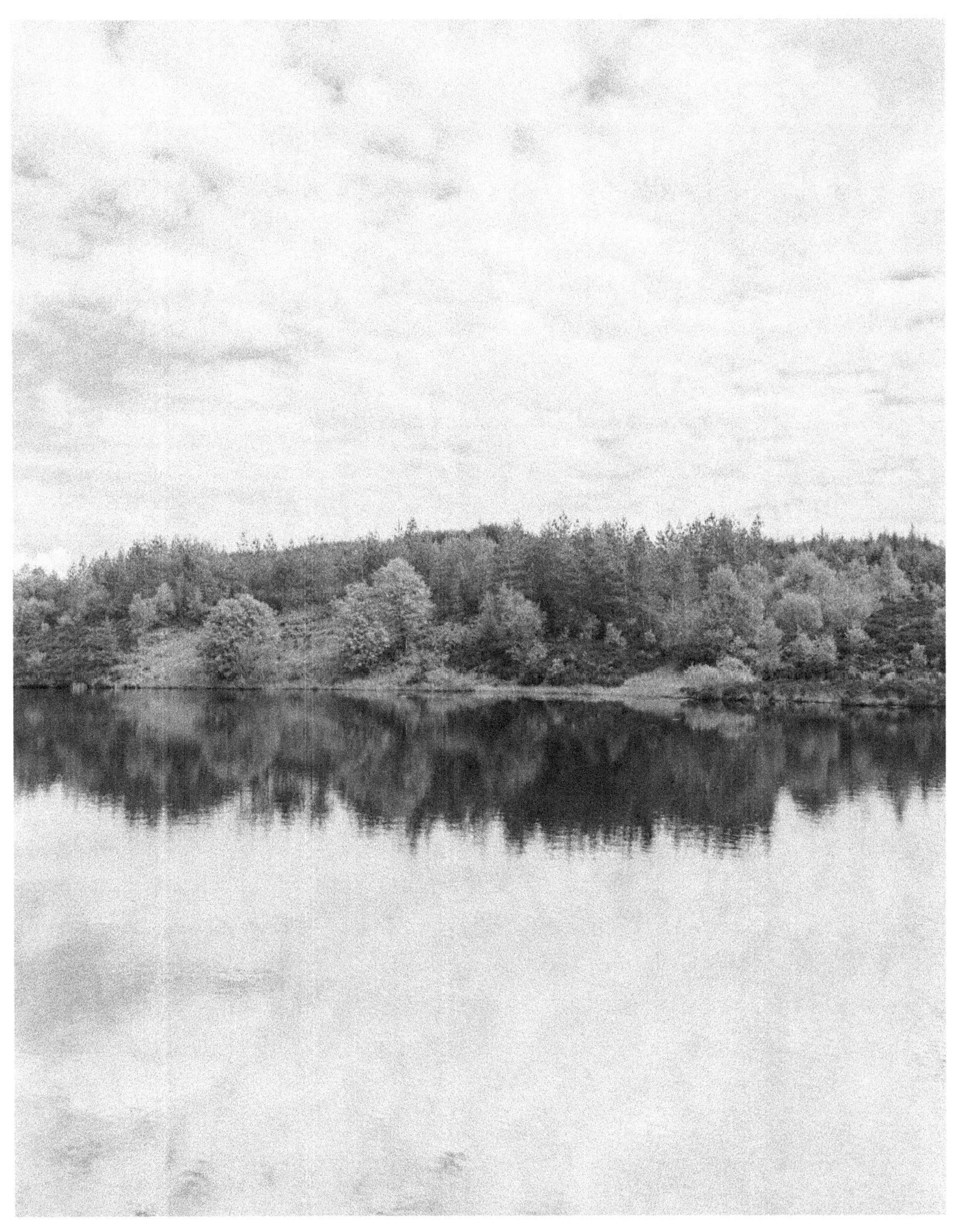

Psalm 32:1–11, NIV

Blessed is the one

    whose transgressions are forgiven,

    whose sins are covered.

Blessed is the one

    whose sin the Lord does not count against them

    and in whose spirit is no deceit.

When I kept silent,

    my bones washed away

    through my groaning all day long.

For day and night

    your hand was heavy on me;

    my strength was sapped

    as in the heat of the summer.

Then I acknowledged my sin to you

    and did not cover up my iniquity.

    I said, "I will confess my transgressions to the Lord."

    And you forgave the guilt of my sin.

Therefore let all the faithful pray to you

> *while you may be found;*

> *surely the rising of the mighty waters will not reach them.*

You are my hiding place;

> *you will protect me from trouble*

> *and surround me with songs of deliverance.*

I will instruct you and teach you in the way you should go;

> *I will counsel you with my loving eye on you.*

Do not be like the horse or the mule,

> *which have no understanding*

> *but must be controlled by bit and bridle*

> *or they will not come to you.*

Many are the woes of the wicked,

> *but the Lord's unfailing love*

> *surrounds the one who trusts him.*

Rejoice in the Lord and be glad, you righteous;

> *sing, all you who are upright in heart!*

My Prayer of Surrendering

Dear God,

Please help me to continue surrendering to Your will. As a line in the poem "Surrender" says, "…change of heart when God's let in." There is a change of heart when we surrender to You. When we follow Your Word, as it is written, our hearts change.

You created everything. You created us. We are here to serve You, our God. Your Word is our guide. I pray to You to help me always have faith and reverence for You. You are my God. You are our God. I pray to You to guide me in helping ones who have not surrendered. I pray to You to help me touch the ones who do not know You. I pray to You to continue to guide me with the words I am writing in these poems and inspirations, and I ask for Your help in sharing these words with others. It is my hope that these words will find ones who have not surrendered and do not know You. And it is my hope that these words touch those who do know You and help them further their faith and love for You.

"My Lord and my God!" John 21:28, NIV

Your loving and devoted son,
Amen

1. If sin is "*anything that would not please God,*" what sin (or sins) do you keep repeating?

2. What part of your soul and heart are not surrendering to God, causing you to repeat these sins?

3. Are you afraid you will lose part of yourself if you fully surrender yourself to God?

4. What are you afraid you will lose?

WORSHIP MUSIC RECOMMENDATIONS

I Surrender • Hillsong Worship
youtube.com/watch?v=s7jXASBWwwI

Abandoned • Benjamin William Hastings & Brandon Lake
youtube.com/watch?v=iRFw9s_cQwE

TODD'S PRAYER

TODD'S PRAYER

"TODD'S PRAYER" is a story about a friend who was inspired by God to answer a prayer—he just did not know whose prayer he was answering. I believe God directs us into situations to guide our lives and also the lives of others. These "life experiences" are steppingstones for our spiritual growth. They are compass coordinates provided by God. I like to say,

"Stop and see what God wants you to see,"

and,

"Stop and listen to what God wants you to hear."

In the chapter titled "Spiritual Renewal," I tell the story of how God put me in a situation to engage with a homeless man at a rest stop. I believe He did this so I could learn to love all my brothers and sisters. But it was my choice to stop and engage with the young man. God provided me with the coordinates, but it was up to me to follow His lead.

In the chapter titled "Finding Home," I relate how God knew that I needed to spend time in a homeless encampment to learn that our physical home is just a place, and that our eternal home is with Him. When we follow God's coordinates we are,

"Stopping to see, or stopping to listen, to what God wants for us."

Sometimes the coordinates God's provides, and the direction they are leading us, can be confusing. If they are, trust in God's leading. God never provides the wrong coordinates. This chapter, "Todd's Prayer" is about a man who was following God's directions and thinking he knew where God was leading him, but in the end, he was completely surprised to where God took him.

Todd's Story

My friend, Todd, and his wife were traveling for a long weekend to see their daughter at college. They had visited her many times while she was away at school. One of their favorite routines was going to the local coffee shop and then to breakfast. One morning at the coffee shop before breakfast, Todd saw a homeless woman sitting at a table, drinking coffee. Todd and his family sat down and drank their coffee and then proceeded to breakfast a few blocks away.

Shortly after being seated in the restaurant, Todd felt a calling from God. He felt God was telling him to go back to the coffee shop and see if he could help the homeless woman. Todd excused himself from the table and said he would be back in a few minutes. He then walked back to the coffee shop.

As he entered the establishment, he noticed that the homeless woman was gone. He went up to the counter and asked the barista who had served him if the homeless woman came to the coffee shop regularly. The barista said, "Yes, she is here most days." Todd asked the barista if he could put some money in an account so the homeless woman's coffee would be paid for, for a few weeks. As Todd was explaining this to the barista, she started to cry. Todd was confused. He asked her why she was crying, she replied, "Earlier today I prayed to God to help that homeless woman."

Todd is a strong Christian and I believe God was asking Todd to help. Todd was following all the coordinates that God was giving him. All the while, as he was following God's lead, Todd felt he was answering a calling from God to help the homeless woman, but God was actually directing him to answer a prayer from the barista, indirectly helping the homeless woman. Imagine if Todd had not gone up to the counter and engaged with the barista. Imagine if he had talked to another barista. Imagine if Todd had resisted God's calling when he was sitting down for breakfast and had not gone back to the coffee shop. *Stop and see, and stop and listen, to what God wants you to experience!*

When I was telling this story to my wife, I was emotionally overwhelmed by the true beauty of this story. Maybe the homeless woman was an angel from God to help Todd build his love and compassion for others. Maybe the barista was an angel from God. One thing I do know, this story is not a coincidence.

God asks us to do things to participate in His mission. It is a privilege to partner with God! If we "stop and see what God wants us to see," we will be answering God's calling. We will be following the co-ordinates that God has provided. In this story, two people were spiritually impacted immediately, Todd and the barista. I also believe God made this happen so Todd could tell his story to others. Retelling this story over and over spreads the Word of God, spiritually impacting more people.

We live in two worlds. First, we live in the physical world of sight, sounds, and touch. We also live in our own very personal spiritual world. As Christians, we pray, we meditate, and we talk to God. When our spiritual beliefs align with our physical world actions, we are living our Christian values. Peace is found when our spiritual beliefs coincide directly with our physical world, thus allowing us to live as sin free as possible. If we were monks, we would spend much of your day sequestered in a monastery, living most of our day in our spiritual world. Each day, our physical world would not change much and there would be very few outside influences, making it easier to live our Christian values. But we are not monks, and our world today makes it difficult to align our Christian spiritual beliefs with our physical world. Daily, we are exposed to sinful temptations. Every day, we need to work hard at making decisions in our physical world that reflect the values of our Christian beliefs.

Todd was following the coordinates God provided him. We are all characters in a beautifully orchestrated play from God, and the Bible is our script. Todd was following God's script. And in doing so, he was perfectly aligning God's spiritual world with his physical world. Todd brought Scripture to life by following the coordinates provided by God. This is the goal that God has for us. Todd was following God's Word.

In Jesus's short time on Earth, He performed may miracles. These occurred in the physical world. These physical world miracles have a parallel spiritual world meaning. Jesus physically provided food for the hungry. If we have faith, we will never go spiritually hungry. Jesus healed the sick. If we have faith, we will never be spiritually sick. Jesus gave sight to the blind. If we have faith, we will always have spiritual sight. We will, in essence, be better able to:

"Stop and see what God wants us to see."

Stop and see. We live in an amazingly beautiful and perfectly designed world. We live in God's physical world. And we live in God's physical world—that is, for a very short time. Enjoy each day; embrace a new, God-inspired "life experience" each day, and follow God's coordinates, wherever they may lead you.

Thank you, God, for guiding us down Your beautiful paths.
We are forever grateful for Your love.

As Jesus approached Jericho, a blind man was sitting by the roadside begging.

When he heard the crowd going by, he asked what was happening.

They told him, "Jesus of Nazareth is passing by."

He called out, "Jesus, Son of David, have mercy on me!"

Those who led the way rebuked him and told him to be quiet,

but he shouted all the more,

"Son of David, have mercy on me!"

Jesus stopped and ordered the man to be brought to him.

When he came near, Jesus asked him, "What do you want me to do for you?"

"Lord, I want to see," he replied.

Jesus said to him, "Receive your sight; your faith has healed you."

Immediately he received his sight and followed Jesus, praising God.

When all the people saw it they also praised God.

My Prayer to Help Us All See the Beauty of Both Our Spiritual and Physical Worlds

Dear God,

You provide us with many signs to help us build our faith in You and in Your Word. Unfortunately, many times we do not see what You want us to see and we do not hear what You want us to hear. "Todd's Prayer" is about a man who listened to You and followed Your direction to answer a prayer. Todd relied on his faith and love of You to answer a prayer, even though whose prayer he was answering was a surprise. As it is written in 1 Corinthians 2:9,

"What no eye has seen,

What no ear has heard,

And what no human mind has conceived

the things God has prepared for those who

love him."

God, we do not know what You have prepared for us. We just need to have faith that whatever Your plan is will be the right plan. I pray that we have the courage and the faith to follow Your direction. I pray that we have the faith to open our eyes and see what You want us to see. I pray that we have the faith to open our ears and hear what You want us to hear.

Your plan for our lives is not a straight line. If Your plan appears crooked, give us the strength to continue to have faith and believe in You. God, please help us align our actions in the physical world with the truths You have taught us in Your Word. Our world has many sinful influences. Please give us strength and faith in You to avoid these influences. You and Your Word are the only answer for our world today.

"My Lord and my God!" John 21:28, NIV

Your loving and devoted son,

Amen

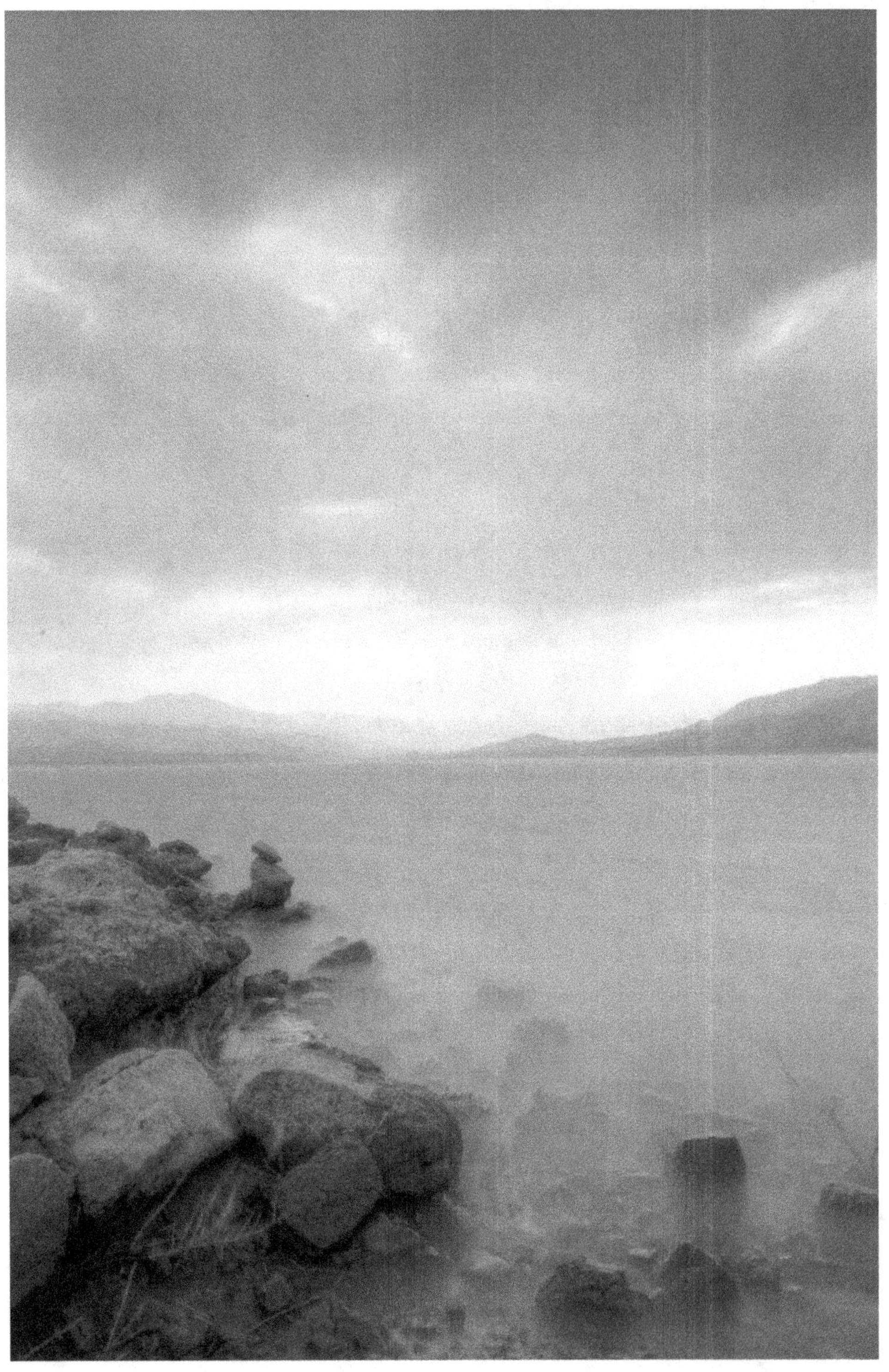

1. How can you change each day so you will "stop and see what God wants you to see, and stop and listen to what God wants you to hear"?

2. Think of a time when you ignored one of God's coordinates. How can you better follow God's coordinates in the future?

3. Like Todd, in "Todd's Prayer," have you ever answered what you felt was a calling from God, following one of God's coordinates? What message do you feel God was sending you?

5. What can you do better to align your physical world with your spiritual world to find the peace and direction that God wants us all to have?

WORSHIP MUSIC RECOMMENDATIONS

You Make Everything Beautiful • Rebecca St. James, for King + Country
youtube.com/watch?v=vTSpGn9-N5Q 

 *Every Good Thing* • Pat Barrett
youtube.com/watch?v=sR7DZIH2z8w

I DON'T KNOW

I DON'T KNOW

A Poem

"I DON'T KNOW" is a story and poem about something that happened to me. I have reflected on it many times, trying to understand what God was telling me. Finally, I realized that we do not always know what God is trying to tell us. In the chapter titled "Todd's Prayer," I wrote about following God's coordinates,

"Sometimes the coordinates God's provides, and the direction they are leading us, can be confusing. If they are, trust in God's leading. God never provides the wrong coordinates."

I imagine our short physical life and journey with God like the "Dot-to Dot" drawing books we had growing up. We would begin at number one and complete the picture many numbers later. It was not until we were about three quarters through that we could visualize what the drawing would be. As Christians and people of faith, this is what our lives are like; we follow God's coordinates wherever they may lead us. If we open our eyes to see what God wants us to see and listen to what God wants us to hear, He will lead us from one number to the next. And as we move from one of God's coordinates to the next, the picture God is painting for us becomes clear. All God wants from us is our faith and love. He wants our obedience, too. Jesus said, "If you love Me, you will do what I command" (John 14:15).

If we have faith and follow God's coordinates wherever they may lead us, God will assist us in painting a masterpiece for our lives.

The Story

For a couple of hours on weekend mornings, I enjoy my quiet time reading the paper and checking emails. Sometimes I will watch and listen to worship music on YouTube. On this particular Saturday morning, my wife was at a conference for the day so I was alone in the house. I started to watch a song on YouTube by Brandon Lake titled, "Talking to Jesus." I do not remember if I had ever heard or watched this song before. Early in the video, I started to focus on the singer and the lyrics in the song. And then I started to become emotional. As the song progressed, I became more emotional and midway through the eight-minute song I was weeping, which continued for the entire video.

This occurred over two years ago and, ever since, I have struggled to try and understand my experience. When I regained my composure, my first thought was, *What just happened and what message was God sending me?* I have replayed it over and over in my mind, trying to understand. Finally, I did understand.

The messages, coordinates, and signals from God are not always clear. This is why it is so important to always have faith. God's directions are God's plan. It is our belief in God and our faith in Him that give us the strength to follow His plan. It is not our plan; it is God's plan.

The song "Talking to Jesus" talks about this, saying that there is no wrong way to do it or bad time to start—that even if it doesn't sound "pretty," we should simply tell Him what's on our heart.

Every one of us can talk to Jesus more. For many people, praying is hard. The word "pray" makes people feel uncomfortable. "Talking to Jesus" sounds easier. We talk to people all the time. It is no different when we are "talking to Jesus."

"Hi, Jesus. How are You? How is Your day? Jesus, what do You think about this? Jesus, I am struggling a little. Jesus, my work is not going well. Jesus, I love You."

"Talking to Jesus" is such a beautiful song. I hope you listen to it over and over. So is the old, classic hymn, "What a Friend We Have in Jesus":

What a friend we have in Jesus,

All our sins and griefs to bear!

What a privilege to carry

Everything to God in prayer!

Oh, what peace we often forfeit,

Oh, what needless pain we bear,

All because we do not carry

Everything to God in prayer!

Have we trials and temptations?

Is there trouble anywhere?

We should never be discouraged—

Take it to the Lord in prayer.

Can we find a friend so faithful,

Who will all our sorrows share?

Jesus knows our every weakness;

Take it to the Lord in prayer.

Are we weak and heavy-laden,

Cumbered with a load of care?

Precious Savior, still our refuge—

Take it to the Lord in prayer.

Do thy friends despise, forsake thee?

Take it to the Lord in prayer!

In His arms He'll take and shield thee,

Thou wilt find a solace there.

~Joseph M. Scriven, 1855

Our journey with God requires us to continually challenge ourselves to go deeper in our relationship with Him. How you challenge yourself to go deeper with Him is up to you. You could listen to worship music more. You could read the Bible more. You could become more involved with your church. Maybe you could just talk to Jesus more. These kinds of efforts build your relationship with God, growing your faith and love for Him. My writings are one of the ways I grow my relationship with God, helping me go deeper to build my faith and love.

The third part of the title of this book, "One Man's Walk with God," is how God views His relationship with you. It is your walk with our Father. It is His coordinates you are following. It is His plan for your life that will unfold.

Do not always look for answers. Focus on God's love and the answers unfold. Follow the "dot-to dots." The picture that God is helping you paint for your life is a beautiful masterpiece.

God,

Thank You for showing me the path and painting my masterpiece.

I DON'T KNOW

God, I gave You my heart

Made Your Son my Savior

I learned of Your Love

And that Grace is forever

Then I learned not to earn

And that Faith is Your favor

But the road that You've shown

Seems crooked and wavered

God, I don't know what direction to go,

But You do

God, I've surrendered my heart

To follow Your Way

I read of Your Word

It's my guide for the day

And my heart's filled with Love

With Faith in Your Way

But the Road still has twists

It's hard to not stray

God, I don't know what direction to go,

But You do

God, with a spirit renewed

And a love for all

The direction I walk

Is the direction You call

Your path is more clear
With a love that's renewed
But there still are the twists
In the fog and the gloom

God, I don't know what direction to go,
But You do

God, You showed me the light
As You directed me home
My path and the road
My picture is shown

The answer is Faith
And a Love that's not hollow
My road still has twists
But a direction to follow

God, I don't know what direction to go,
But You do

God, my life is for You
And my guide is Your Way
My path may be clouded
But my Faith will not stray

With Faith and Love
Your direction is clear
My picture You paint
Of a home that's so near

God, I don't know what direction to go,
But You do

Proverbs 3:5–6, NIV

Trust in the Lord with all your heart

and lean not on your own understanding;

in all your ways submit to him,

and he will make your paths straight.

Psalm 32:8-9, NIV

I will instruct you and teach you in the way you should go;

I will counsel you with my loving eye on you.

Do not be like the horse or the mule,

which have no understanding but must be controlled by bit and bridle

or they will not come to you.

My Prayer to Help Us Build Our Faith and Love in God Knowing That He Will Be the Guide in Our Paths

Dear God,

Your Word is our guide. It is our Faith in You and Your Word that helps us follow the path that You are guiding for our lives. God, following this path can be hard. When we waver from this path, we need to remember Your Word and that our lives are in Your hands. Your love for us is so strong and unconditional that it is hard to fully comprehend.

God, please give me and all those reading this the strength each day to not waver from Your Word and the path You have for us. God, please help those that do not know Your path to learn of Your love and build their faith in Your way. Help them find their path with You. God, please help those that believe in You but are confused in the direction You are leading them to continue to believe and have faith. Your path is not straight, but it is the plan You have for us, and as our lives unfold, the picture becomes clearer.

God, thank You for the unconditional and endless love You pour out on us, and the grace You grant us even when we waver from the path You have for our lives. As sinners, it is Your grace and love for us that gives us redemption and eternal life with You.

"My Lord and my God!" John 21:28, NIV

Your loving and devoted son,
Amen

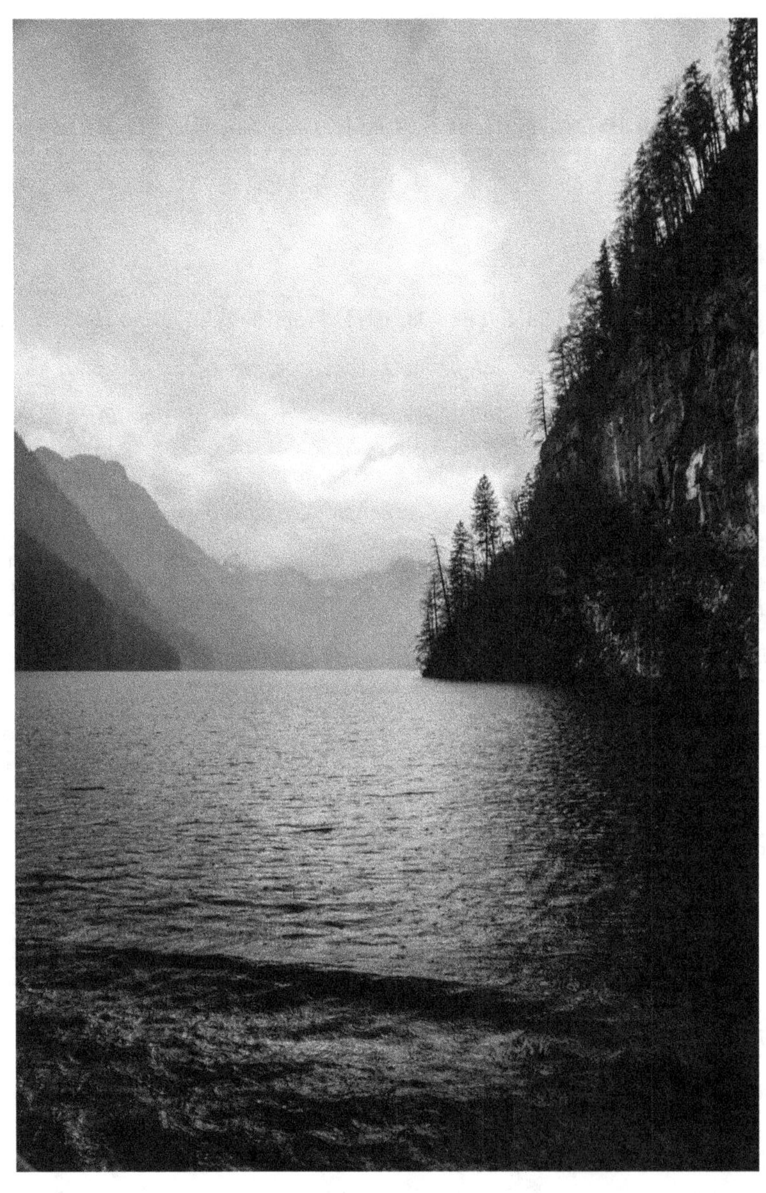

Reflections for Your Journey

1. Has there been a time when you had to stop and think, *What is God trying to tell me or why is God lead-ing me this way?* If you followed God's path, what message do think God was sending you?

2. Our faith in God can be challenged through the difficult times in life—issues such as the death of a loved one, health and job concerns, or injustices we may suffer. It is often said that God will not give us more than we can handle. Why do you think God allows us to be challenged in these difficult times?

3. What is one thing you can change in your life and your relationship with God so you can better follow the "dot-to-dots" as you and God paint the masterpiece of your life?

4. Reflect on this verse: "And we know that in all things God works for the good of those who love him, who have been called according to his purpose" (Romans 8:29). How does this biblical truth encourage you?

WORSHIP MUSIC RECOMMENDATIONS

Talking to Jesus • Brandon Lake, Elevation Worship & Maverick City
youtu.be/OXsxw1fRHMA?si=WoOgtWeElBcDaqN2 

 *What a Friend We Have in Jesus* • Alan Jackson
youtu.be/znWu2HCJ92c?si=rju7mQSvKqS1Z0f0

DEAR GOD

DEAR GOD

A Poem

SOMETIMES IT IS HARD to keep our faith in God when we see so much hurt and pain in the world. "Dear God" is the fifth poem I wrote. My knowledge about Scripture and the history of biblical writings is limited. There is so much to learn. The poem was written when I was questioning, "Why is the world like it is? Why is it not better? Why is there not more peace and love?"

My pastor gave a sermon that helped to answer these questions. The sermon was about how God has given us free will. He gives us the ability to choose. God does not want to control His children. He wants His children to make their own decisions and govern themselves in their own way.

We have the freedom to choose between right and wrong and between sinning and not sinning. God's plan has always been to give us the freedom to choose. God is observing our choices. He is observing our choices as individuals and as a society. God will only intervene when He feels He needs to.

He may cure someone of cancer. He may nudge someone toward becoming born again. He may change the direction of society. God was so frustrated with the Jewish people not listening to His Word that He expelled them from their homeland for two thousand years.

In many ways, how we treat each other and how our governing bodies have ruled hasn't changed much. The evil in the world today is no different than the evil of two thousand years ago. Evil is evil and sin is sin. Interestingly, the last words in the Lord's Prayer are:

"Deliver us from evil."

With our freedom to choose comes a responsibility to God. We have a responsibility to follow His Word and have faith. Although we will sin, and God knows we will sin, every day we need to try hard to not sin. We live in a world where sin resides, and evil resides. God is watching us, and He is watching how hard we try not to sin.

God has a plan, and we need to have unwavering faith that God's plan is the right plan and the only plan. Having faith and keeping our faith is very difficult. We cannot touch faith, we cannot hold faith, and we cannot measure faith. Faith is intangible. Faith requires an unwavering belief in the Word of God.

God is recruiting an All-Star Team for the afterlife. Have faith and try hard not to sin so you can be on the team.

God, I do understand.

DEAR GOD

The ways of the world seem evil and cruel

Villains of times are forceful and rule

Why do we hunger for food and shelter

Why do we dream of life there after

You sent us Your Son to teach of Love

You sent us Your Son to believe in above

Do we follow the path that Jesus preached

Or do we follow the path of evil's reach

You sent us Your Son to teach of Peace

But, I see no Peace

Has anything changed in two thousand years

Are we still afraid with similar fears

Dear God…I do not understand

Was the message that Jesus conveyed

That nothing would change, as long as we stayed

And being of flesh, means we will always be

But having Faith allows us to see

Eternal Life and Peace from above

Comes with our Faith and Faith in His Love

And with this Faith we become God's kin

And then and forever He forgives our sins

It seems so easy, but it is so hard

Without Faith and Love, eternal life is barred

Dear God…I do understand.

We know that the law is spiritual; but I am unspiritual, sold as a slave to sin. I do not understand what I do. For what I want to do I do not do, but what I hate I do. And If I do what I do not want to do, I agree that the law is good. As it is, it is no longer I myself who do it, but it is sin living in me. For I know that good itself does not dwell in me, that is, in my sinful nature. For I have the desire to do what is good, but I cannot carry it out. For I do not do the good I want to do, but the evil I do not want to do—this I keep doing. Now if I do what I want to do, it is no longer I who do it, but it is sin living within me that does it.

My Prayer for All of Us to Ask God to Give Us Strength to Not Sin and When We Do Sin to Confess Our Sins to Him

Dear God,

Why, in the world we live in, is it so hard to not sin? As Romans 7:15 says,"I do not understand what I do. For what I want to do I do not do, but what I hate I do."

God, it is so hard to understand why we sin and why we keep sinning. I understand that sin is in our world and that people will sin, but why do I keep sinning? It does not seem right to just accept that we will sin and when we do sin, to just ask for Your forgiveness.

It is hard to accept that I will continue to sin as long as I live on Earth, and that when I am accepted into Heaven, I will no longer sin. I am disappointed when I sin because I know that I have disappointed You.

Believe me, God, when I say,"I do not want to be a sinner." Your love for us is so strong that when we do sin, You forgive us. This is the "Amazing Grace" You give to all Your children. God, please give me and all Your believers the strength we need. Give us the strength to press into our faith. Give us the strength to press into Your Word every day.

We are Your children, and we live for You.

"My Lord and my God!" John 21:28, NIV

Your loving and devoted son,

Amen

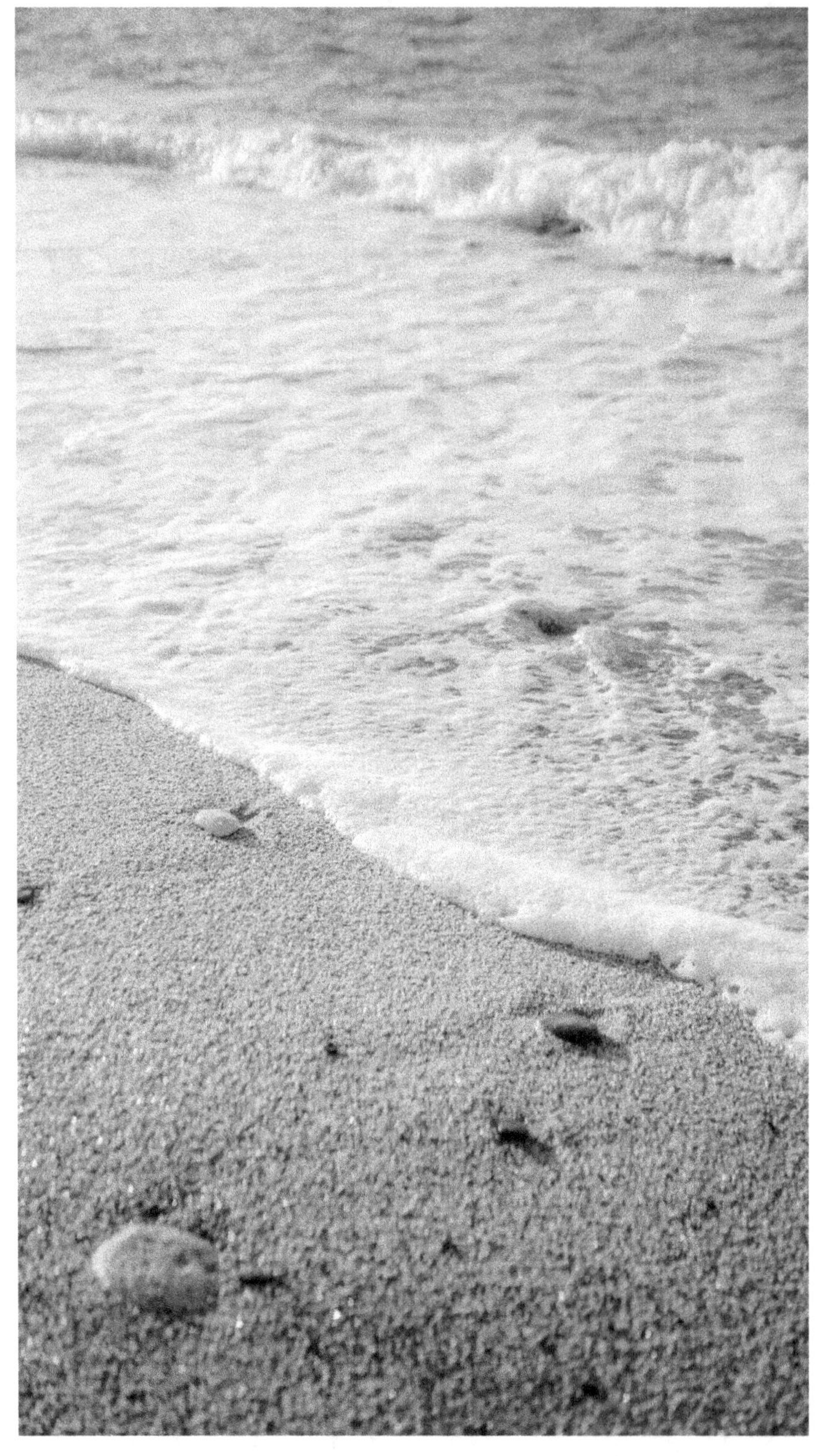

1. Think of someone you've observed who has a hard time resisting sinful temptations. Then think of someone you've observed who has experienced victory in this area. What can you learn from their experiences so you can better resist sinful temptations?

2. Why do you think Jesus used the words, "Deliver us from evil" in the Lord's Prayer?

3. Why do you think God gives us the freedom to choose?

4. When we do choose the wrong path, what do you think is God's response to us when we repent and turn back to Him? Read Psalm 103:8–14 with this in mind. What do you learn about God's character in this passage?

WORSHIP MUSIC RECOMMENDATIONS

Oh but God • Davy Flowers
youtube.com/watch?v=8ebRIca4PGU

Joy in the Morning • Tauren Wells, Elevation Worship
youtube.com/watch?v=uysGt7JVw9U

MY HEART ACHES

MY HEART ACHES

A Poem

BECOMING A BORN-AGAIN CHRISTIAN has brought so much peace and love into my heart—so much so, I want everyone to feel the same peace and love. Maybe that is why God wants us to be disciples of His Word.

The poem "My Heart Aches" is about hoping these feelings of peace and love will be felt by someone who continues to question their faith. This is the sixth poem I wrote, and it is about a friend of mine.

They struggle with their faith. They believe in God, but I think they are afraid of God. They are afraid to live the life that God wants us to live. It is like they are on the top of a fence with one leg in God's backyard and the other leg in Satan's backyard. They are not unique with these feelings. Many people question God's Word. And when you question God's Word, you are questioning your faith. Below is a verse from my poem "Afraid":

"But I am afraid to bare my soul to a God I do not know."

I think this is how many others feel. Do not be afraid. God loves you.

People who are afraid of God have not truly felt the peace and love that God's Word brings. I pray for people who are afraid of God. My friend is young, immature, and still susceptible to ungodly influences. They have so much good inside of them and I feel that God's path for my friend is to help others heal and find the Word of God. My friend has the talent to be a very powerful disciple for God if they choose to be. My role is to love and support.

The poem is also about how hard it is to really help someone when they are not ready to heal themselves. Childhood trauma creates many wounds. If these wounds are not treated, they scab over, and scabs can easily come off, reopening wounds. The Word turns a scabbed wound into a scarred wound. You know the wound is still there, but because of the scar, it is more protected.

God's Word heals us. It is God's Word that gives us the support to make sure the scar is secure, and the wound does not reopen. Fully healing scabbed, emotional wounds from childhood trauma is painful and unfortunately too often avoided.

Avoid no more.

Being young is difficult. Finding our path in life is hard. God helps make finding our path easier. Bringing the Word of God to young people is a powerful and life-changing gift.

My poetry is a gift to myself, but I hope it is also a gift to others. This poem is a gift from me to her with the hope that it will make her path a little easier to follow.

I pray for my friend often.

MY HEART ACHES

I feel her hurt and she feels pain,
I see her loneliness, she drift … the same

I feel her hide and scared to share,
She lives alone afraid to bare

My heart aches for one I love

I feel her asking, "Why … where do I go"
I see her lost and wandering so

I feel her question our God above
I see her closing God's book of Love

My heart aches for one I love

I feel my heart wander too
As she stumbles and drifts away from you

I too feel lost at where to go
I see her thinking, she does not know

My heart aches for one I love

I feel the hope You give with prayer
She tries so hard, but sees despair

I feel and pray that time will heal
I see her try to learn, to love, to know You're real

My heart aches for one I love

God, give her time to work things out
She is still lost … and wanders about

1 John 1:8–10, NIV

If we claim to be without sin, we deceive ourselves and the truth is not in us. If we confess our sins, he is faithful and just and will forgive us our sins and purify us from all unrighteousness. If we claim we have not sinned, we make him out to be a liar and his word is not in us.

John 16:33 NIV

"I have told you these things, so that in me you may have peace. In this world you will have trouble. But take heart! I have overcome the world."

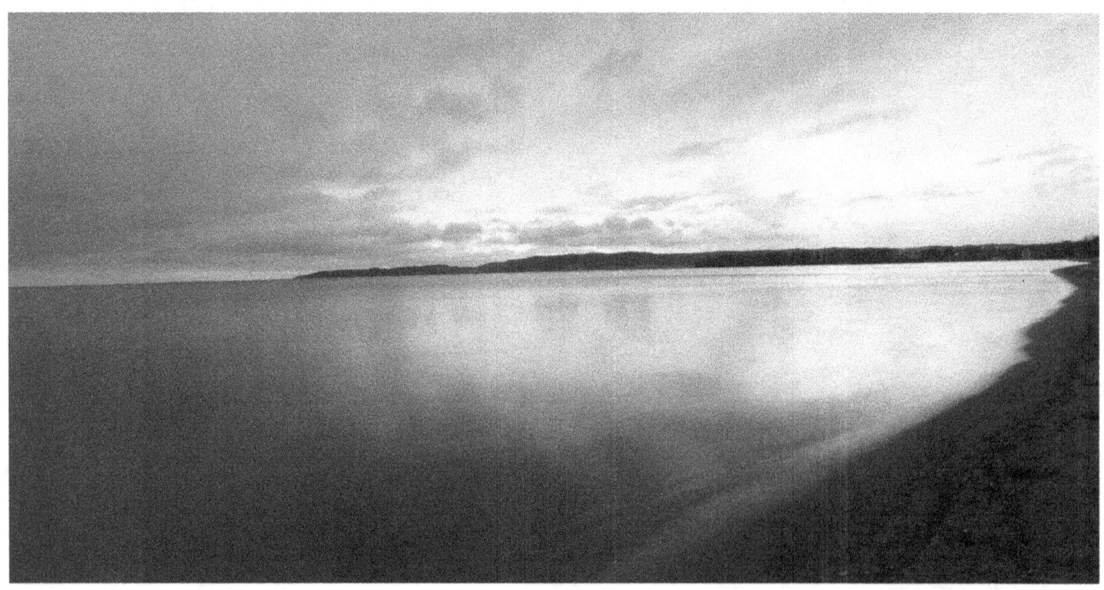

My Prayer for Her and Others Who Struggle with Their Faith

Dear God,

We all struggle with difficult feelings and emotions. That is why faith in You and faith in Your Word is so important. Your power and the power of the Word and the power of faith can heal anything we struggle with.

My friend, for whom this poem is written, struggles with emotional issues. We all have emotional battles we fight. They believe in You, but they have not spent enough time in Your Word to fully understand its healing power.

Like all of us, they are easily tempted by sin. They do not have enough faith or enough understanding of the Word to fully battle sin. Please God, for my friend and others in the same spot, give them the strength to press into Your Word. Please God, give them the patience to learn about the amazing healing power of Your Word. And please God, give them the patience to know that healing takes time. God, You are why we are here and everything we have is because of You.

"My Lord and my God!" John 21:28, NIV

Your loving and devoted son,
Amen

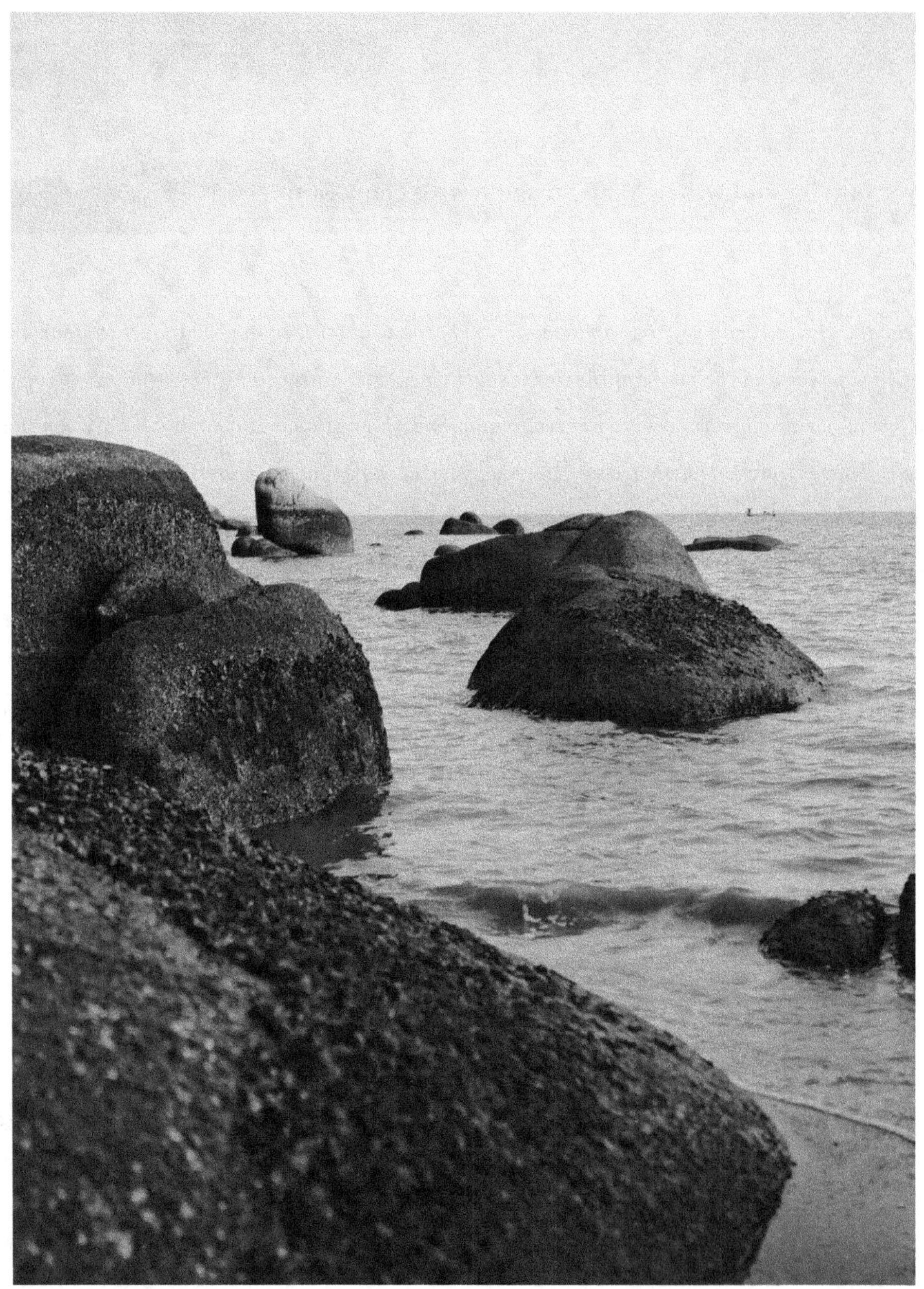

1. Think of someone you know who is struggling. How can you help them find the peace and love that faith in God provides?

2. One of the most rewarding experiences we can have in life is bring someone to our Lord and Savior, Jesus Christ. What can you do to be a soul-winning disciple for our Lord?

3. Many of us have been emotionally hurt by traumatic events from our childhood. If this is true for you, how has your faith in our Lord Jesus Christ helped you deal with this trauma?

4. If you have not dealt with these traumatic wounds, they are still just a scab covering the wound. What are some steps you can take to move out in your faith in God to help you heal these wounds?

WORSHIP MUSIC RECOMMENDATIONS

You're Gonna Be Okay • Jenn Johnson
youtube.com/watch?v=kLiuYPR4YpA

Don't Believe Them • Lauren Daigle
youtube.com/watch?v=jJxy9F4iW0w

I TRY TO LIVE LIKE JESUS

I TRY TO LIVE LIKE JESUS

A Poem

I HAD THE INSPIRATION to write my seventh poem after a Bible study class. We were having an open discussion about living a good Christian life, being kind, being careful how we spoke, and loving God and our neighbors. I started to think how, with our hectic, fast-paced lives, it is hard to live like Jesus. It doesn't matter if we are living now or two thousand years ago, living like Jesus is hard.

I also started to think that, to live like Jesus, we need to search for the peace that Jesus preached of. Finding peace is as hard as living like Jesus. Living like Jesus takes work every day. Finding peace takes work every day.

Living like Jesus and finding peace are related. The more we live like Jesus, the more peace we find. How we interact with others is our calling card, our public expression of our inner peace. Peace is not found in material items. Too often material items become elevated in our lives to a point of worship, or becoming our own pagan gods.

The peace we seek comes from "The Word," written by God for His children. Studying the Word is a lifelong journey, and the Word will never be fully comprehended until we see the beauty and love of God our Father face to face in Heaven.

Every day we are faced with temptations. Living like Jesus and studying the Bible are hard work. Bringing God into everything we think and do is hard work, but the reward is a life of peace and eternal life with God our Father.

I wrote this poem to be read as a fun and lighthearted poem. If you read it to an audience, you could even have the audience participate. The reader of the poem would read each verse and then read the first half of the line, "I try to live like Jesus…" and, out loud, the audience would say:

"But life gets in the way."

I hope you enjoy the poem and read it in the lighthearted way it was written.

God,
Thank You for having a sense of humor.

I TRY TO LIVE LIKE JESUS

I get up in the morning

To start a brand-new day

Rest was good, except when not

Pass the coffee, it should brighten up my way

The paper came, but it's all wet

The dog went out, now she's all wet

The hot water's gone, now I'm all wet

The day just started, don't worry, it's no sweat

I try to live like Jesus…but life gets in the way

The car won't start,

What, the battery's dead

Do I call my boss

Or crawl back into bed

I'll take the bus, that will work

When does it come

What?

I need to download an app

I try to live like Jesus…but life gets in the way

The bus is here

It's early at seven forty-eight

If I run, I'll make it

And won't be late

What, the bus didn't stop

I figured so

The app said third

Now where do I go

I try to live like Jesus…but life gets in the way

At work at last

It's feels good to sit

I'll just do my work

Be calm and have no fits

What?

That's not me. I never said what he said to me

That boss of mine, OMG

Help me, God, to live like Thee

I try to live like Jesus…but life gets in the way

Philippians 4:4–7, NIV

Rejoice in the Lord always. I will say it again: Rejoice! Let your gentleness be evident to all. The Lord is near. Do not be anxious about anything, but in every situation, by prayer and petition, with thanksgiving, present your request to God. And the peace of God, which transcends all understanding, will guard your hearts and your minds in Christ Jesus.

Psalm 56:3, NIV

When I am afraid, I put my trust in you.

My Prayer to Remind Us to Put Our Lives in the Hands of God

Dear God,

I do try to live like Jesus, but as the poem says, "Life Gets in the Way." It is work reminding ourselves to live like Jesus. When I sin, I am sorry. When I forget about You, I am sorry. When I am impatient, I am sorry. When I succumb to temptation, I am sorry. When I forget to study the Word, I am sorry. Please help to remind me and others of the importance to live our lives like Jesus. Please help to remind me and others of the importance to press into Your Word. Pressing into You, trying hard to live like Jesus, and studying the Word will bring us the peace You wish us to have.

Our lives are in Your hands. You are our Father and we are Your children. We are here to live our lives with You as our guide, following Your Word and waiting for the day when we will live with You for eternity in Heaven.

"My Lord and my God!" John 21:28, NIV

Your loving and devoted son,
Amen

Reflections for Your Journey

1. How does your life get in the way of "living like Jesus"?

2. What is one thing you can do or change in your life to live more like Jesus?

3. What is one thing you currently do that brings you God's peace?

4. "I Try to Live Like Jesus" talks about how important it is to study God's Word. Do you have a daily Bible study routine?

WORSHIP MUSIC RECOMMENDATIONS

Reason • Unspoken

youtube.com/watch?v=n3vTmjcv1fk

DON'T CRY

DON'T CRY

A Poem

BOTH OF OUR DAUGHTERS are such beautiful people. They are so accomplished. Their mother and I are so proud of them both. Our oldest daughter, who inspired this poem, left home after graduating from high school and has lived in New York City for over fifteen years. New York is a fun city to visit but I imagine it would be a hard place to live. She has done very well establishing herself in the big city. She has a wonderful group of friends; she met her husband in New York, and has worked her way to the top of her profession.

Every one of us struggles with insecurities or emotional issues. Many times, these struggles are our own personal emotional secrets. I am not sure if it is good or bad to have these secrets. It is what it is. I feel these emotional secrets are more difficult for our oldest daughter, but she accepts them and does well managing them. She has always been very mature with accepting her emotional secrets. I call our emotional secrets our "handicaps," and our handicaps are with us our entire life. We need to learn how to manage our handicaps every day. A quote attributed to Shakespeare says, "We are molded by our faults."

"Don't Cry" is about accepting who we are. God made us. God made us who we are. Everyone has emotional secrets, handicaps, and faults. Jesus Christ is the only perfect individual who has ever lived. And God's Word is the only guide we need to live our lives.

For me, committing my life to God and giving my love to God has helped me manage my emotional secrets and handicaps. It has helped me know why I am here. I am here to serve God in the way I know God wants me to serve Him. God's Word is called "the Way" because it is THE Way!

It is the only way for us to live our lives. I hope this poem helps my beautiful daughter look deeper into "the Way." And I hope it helps you manage your emotional secrets and faults. As a line in the poem says, *"We are who we are."*

God, thank You for loving us. Please help guide my beautiful daughter to Your way.

DON'T CRY

Don't cry, sweet child,
We are who we are
We are what God made us
An image from afar

Comprehending His love
Is the challenge we face
A power, a force
But a power with grace

We are who we are
God made it so
You are the child He envisioned
Don't worry … let go

Trust in His strength
And trust in His love
God is almighty
Our gift from above

You are a gift to Him
Don't try to change
Be just who you are
A child in God's name

Your worries are His
And your troubles too
Trust in our Lord
For He trusts in you

We all struggle
That's why "the Word" is "the Way"
Give your heart to our Father
And to His Son, our Savior, each and
every day

Psalm 40:1–8, NIV

I waited patiently for the Lord;

he turned to me and heard me cry.

He lifted me out of the slimy pit,

out of the mud and the mire;

he set my feet on a rock

and gave me a firm place to stand.

He put a new song in my mouth,

a hymn of praise to our God.

Many will see and fear the Lord

and put their trust in him.

Blessed is the one

who trusts in the Lord,

who does not look to the proud,

to those who turn aside to the false gods.

Many, Lord my God,

Are the wonders you have done,

the things you planned for us.

None can compare to you;

were I to speak and tell of the deeds,

they would be too many to declare.

Sacrifice and offering you did not desire

but my ears you have opened

burnt offerings and sin offering you did not require.

Then I said,"Here I am, I have come—

It is written about me in the scroll.

I desire to do your will, my God;

your law is within my heart."

My Prayer Asking God to Help Us Remember That "We Are Who We Are"

Dear God,

We are who we are. You made us the way we are for the reasons You chose. We should not question those reasons. We should accept ourselves. We are Your vision. If we feel we need to make changes in our lives, Your Word should be our guide. Our emotional secrets and faults usually come from not following Your Word. Please give us strength to everyday press into Your Word and use it as our guide to better our lives. It is when we are not pressing into Your Word that we question who we are and dwell on our faults and handicaps. Give us the strength to devote our lives to Your Word so we can fulfill the design You have for us as Your children. And give us the strength to not question the direction You have planned for our lives. We are here to serve You.

"My Lord and my God!" John 21:28, NIV

Your loving and devoted son,
Amen

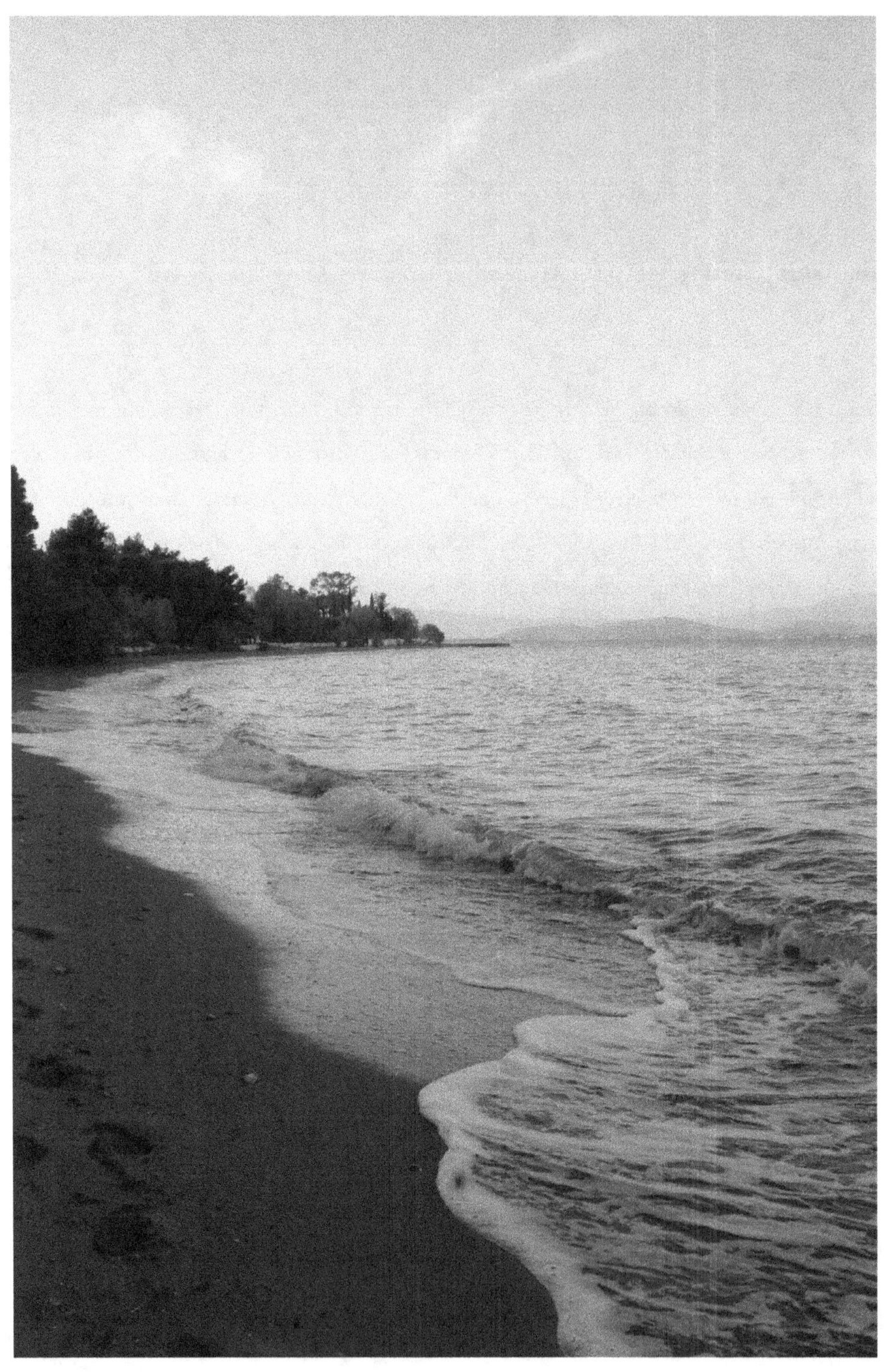

Reflections for Your Journey

1. Do you think it is good or bad to have "emotional secrets"? Why?

2. Would it help you if you talked about your emotional secrets with a friend, pastor, or confidant?

3. What do you feel about the quote attributed to Shakespeare that "we are molded by our faults"?

4. As two lines in the poem say,
    "We are who we are
    God made it so"
    Do you accept who you are?

WORSHIP MUSIC RECOMMENDATIONS

Be Alright • Evan Craft, KB & Sam Rivera
youtube.com/watch?v=SY8lHw218jM 

 *Hold On* • Katy Nichole
youtube.com/watch?v=fxjofrjnfXU

BROKEN

BROKEN

A Poem

I WAS INSPIRED to write this poem when driving on a very busy arterial street in Tacoma. The street has many stop lights and speeds never exceeding twenty-five to thirty miles per hour. Up ahead, on the other side of the street, in an open field which contained old industrial equipment, I saw an overweight woman making erratic movements. The slang word would be "tweaking." She appeared high on drugs. So sad. There is so much drug addiction today. As I drove closer to her, I could see that, other than a large scarf wrapped around her mid-section, she was completely naked. She was exposing her broken and naked soul for all to see.

Broken——is there any other way to describe her? Is there any other way to describe what many of us see every day with the drugs and homelessness in our cities. Saying that these "children of God" are hurting our cities with their garbage and homeless encampments is true, but it would be insensitive to the real issue that these people are broken, maybe so broken that they will never be right.

Their brokenness exposes the spiritual nakedness of our world today.

In some way, we are all broken. We all sin. We all need the grace of God for our own personal redemption. There is a thin line between being who we are and someone whose brokenness takes over their lives. Temptation and sin affect us all. How some of us manage and others do not is a question for God, but having God as our personal Savior, and, every day, living our lives as a child of God, is necessary to help us not be broken.

I also know that if we are broken, God can help. God provides no guarantees to how our lives will be. We are the masters of our ships. The only guarantee we receive from God is that He will love us unconditionally and that He will forgive our sins.

The poem "Broken," my ninth poem, was written from the perspective of someone who is broken, angry, and lost. They are mad, confused, and do not know where to turn. They think that, *maybe*, turning to God will be the answer, but they are not sure.

I am sure. I know God can heal broken souls. Is this the point in the naked, homeless woman's life when she will change? We all have our own brokenness. Reach out to God and pray. He is listening.

Thank You, God, for listening and healing broken souls.

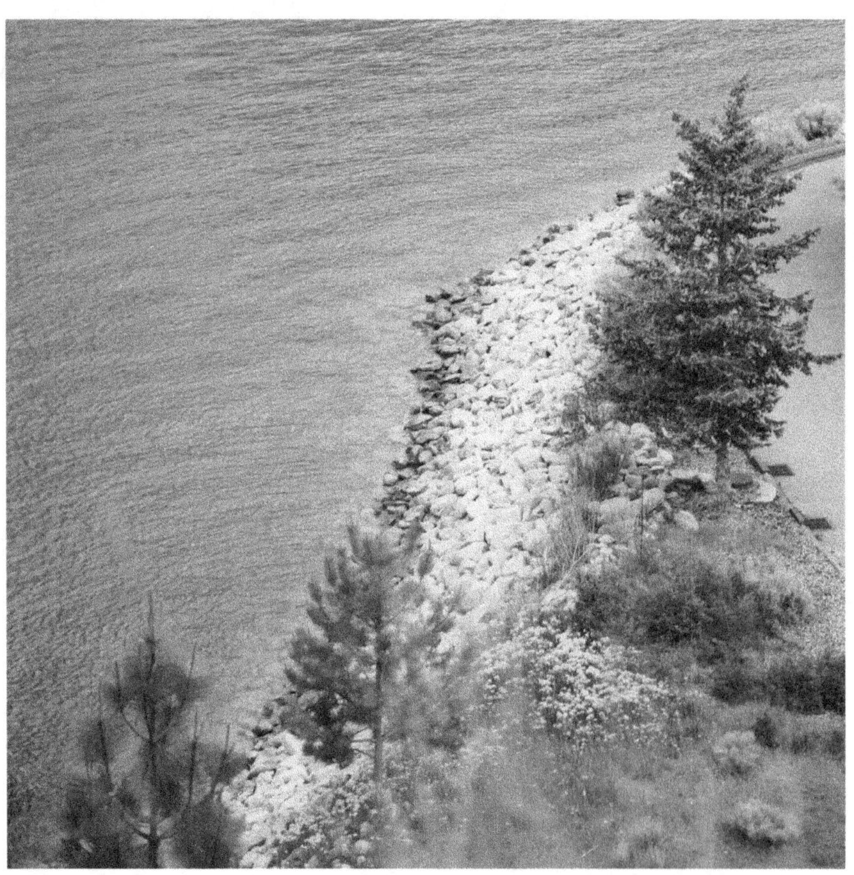

BROKEN

God, why am I broken
I stand here confused
I stand here exposed
I stand here without a soul

> What happened, God
> What went wrong
> What have I done
> God, why am I broken

Where am I, God
Where did I come from
Where do I go
God, please tell me: why am I broken

Why …
Why did I not say no
Why is there no help
Why am I always so cold

> God, when did it start
> When will it stop
> When will I remember
> Please help me … I can go
> no further

Please help me, God

Today I exposed … naked to All

Today I exposed … a naked Soul

Today I exposed … a naked life … hopeless

        Please help me, God, it's time

        I can dig no more

        I can be soulless no more

        I can be lonely no more

Today's the day, I give to You

Today's the day, I say no more

Today's the day

Please help me, God … Let's pray

God…will tomorrow be new

Will tomorrow bring answers

Will I start tomorrow

Tomorrow … tomorrow, God … I promise

        Please help me, God

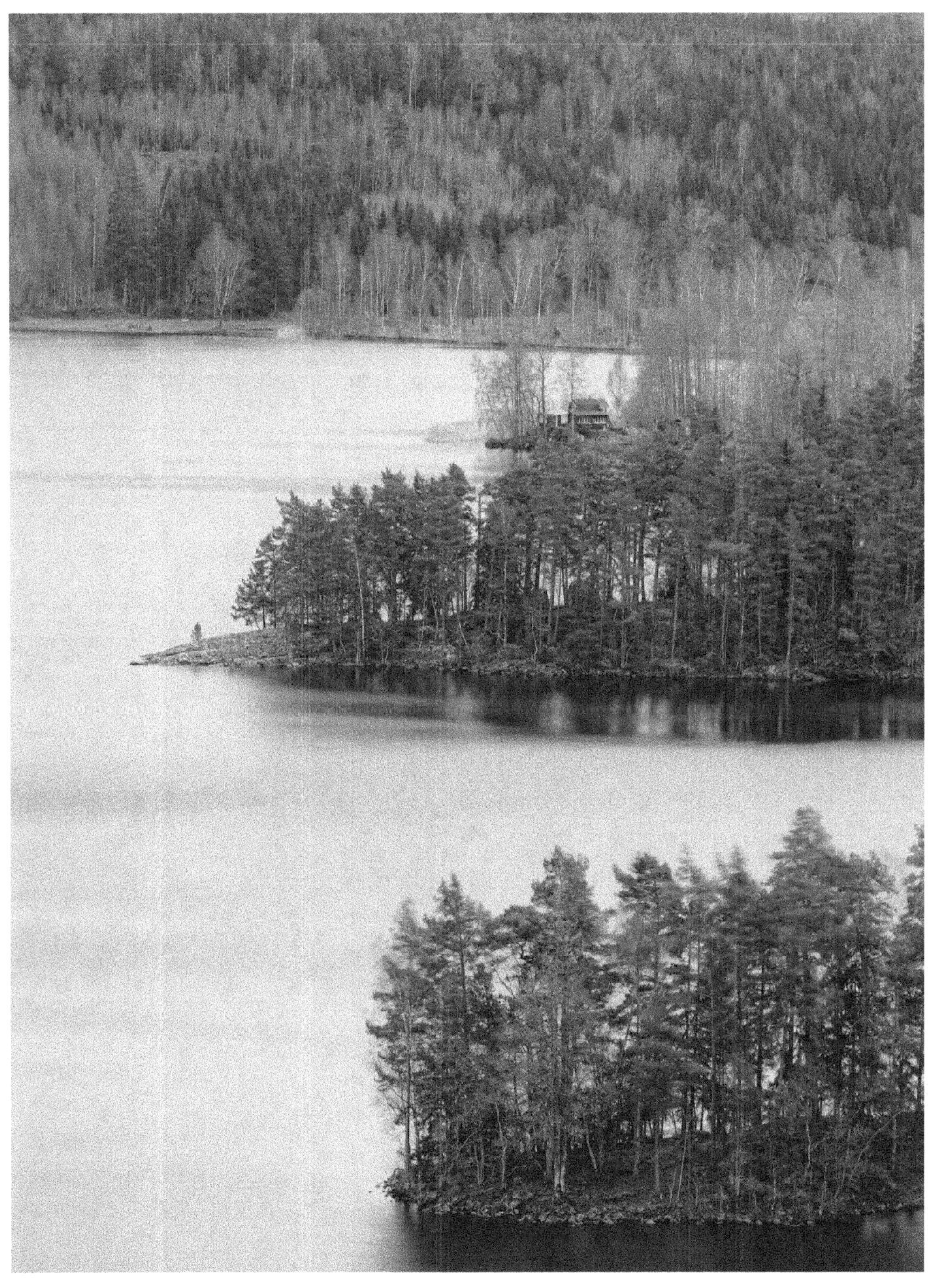

Matthew 5:3–12, NIV

THE BEATITUDES

Blessed are the poor in spirit,

for theirs is the kingdom of heaven.

Blessed are those who mourn,

for they will be comforted.

Blessed are the meek,

for they will inherit the earth.

Blessed are those who are hunger and thirst for righteousness,

for they will be filled.

Blessed are the merciful,

for they will be shown mercy.

Blessed are the pure in heart,

for they will see God.

Blessed are the peacemakers,

for they will be called children of God.

Blessed are those who are persecuted because of righteousness,

for theirs is the kingdom of heaven.

Blessed are you when people insult you,

persecute you and falsely say all kinds of evil against you because of me.

Rejoice and be glad, great is your reward in heaven...

My Prayer for All, for We Are All Broken

Dear God,

In some way, we are all broken. We are all sinners. You sent us Your only Son to die on the cross so our sins would be forgiven. This is the grace You provide to all of us, Your children. Every day we need to try not to sin, to not be broken. We live in a sinful world—a world in which every day we are confronted with temptations to sin. I pray for us to be strong and follow Your Word.

Please never stop giving us Your grace as we confess our sins. Please help the ones like the woman in the poem "Broken," who are truly lost. Help them find You so they can confess their sins and start to heal. The only answer for their lives is You. The only answer for all our lives is You. Please guide us so we can help others, like the woman in the poem, find their way. Please help us to always have compassion for the poor and less fortunate. We are Your children, and we are also disciples of Your Word. We pray that we never forget that we are in Your beautiful world for a short time. It is Your compassion and grace, and our faith, that will allow us to spend eternity with You in Heaven.

"My Lord and my God!" John 21:28, NIV

Your loving and devoted son,
Amen

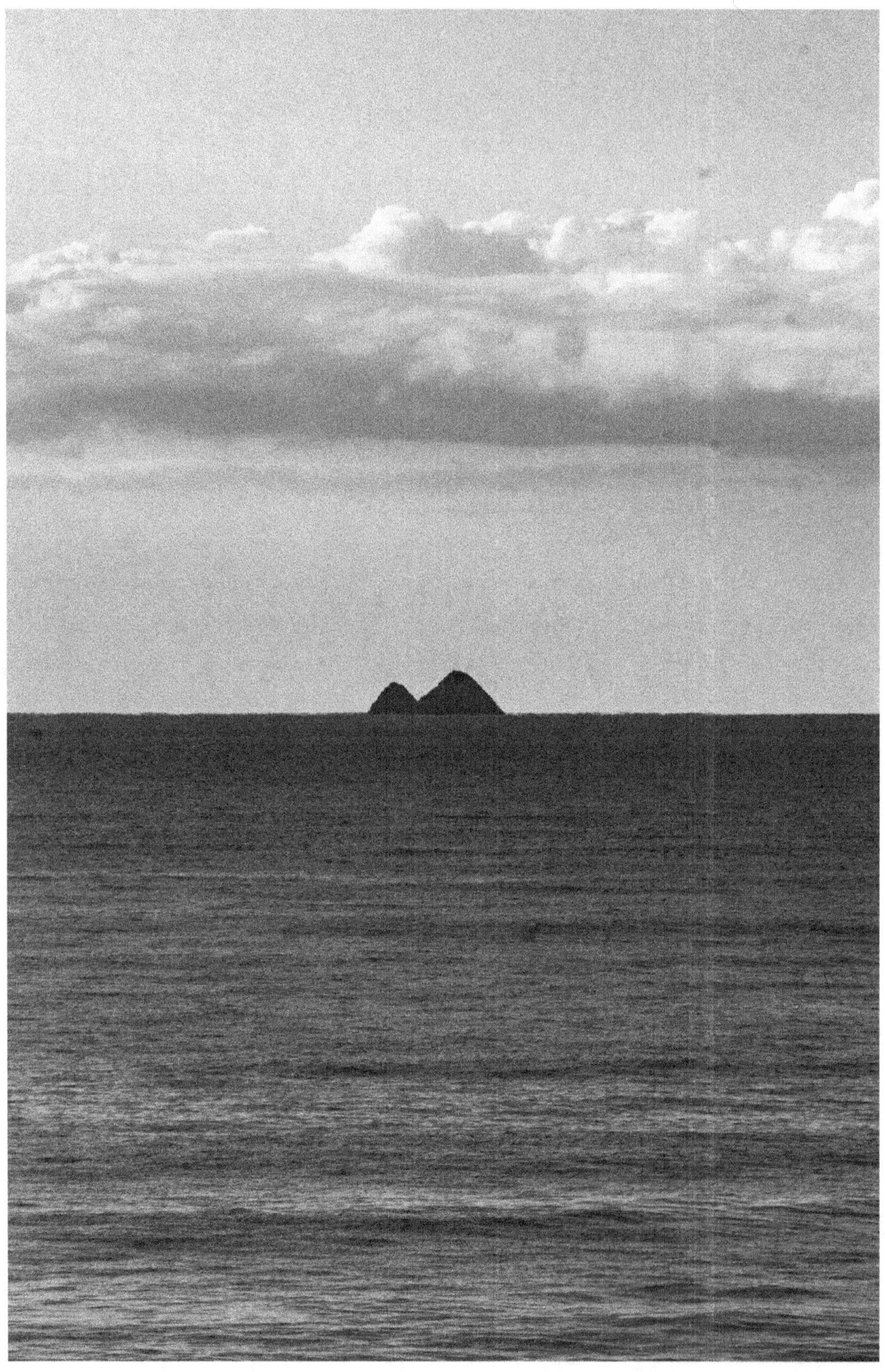

Reflections for Your Journey

1. We are all broken, "for we all have sinned and fall short of the glory of God" (Romans 3:23, NIV). When you think about it, is there any way you expose your broken and naked soul for all to see? Or do you keep it well-hidden? How?

2. Do you accept that the grace of God is the only personal redemption for your sins?

3. The woman in the poem is described as "broken." Is she more broken than you or me? How?

4. Do you believe the "spiritual nakedness of our world today" is greater than in the past? Why or why not?

WORSHIP MUSIC RECOMMENDATIONS

Back to God • Reba McEntire & Lauren Daigle
youtube.com/watch?v=ZoJYF5kD5cA 

 *Help Is on the Way* • TobyMac
youtube.com/watch?v=aVgetIvEIAs

GRACE

GRACE

An Inspiration

GOD'S GRACE IS SAID to be "undeserved favor." And, it is through our faith in the Lord Jesus Christ that we receive God's grace. It is by God's grace that our sins are forgiven.

As Christians, we understand grace and thank God for His grace. But many times, we forget to give ourselves grace. Just as God forgives us, we must also forgive ourselves. We are sinners and every day we are tempted with sin. When we sin, we need to confess our sin to God, forgive ourselves, and give ourselves grace. As Christians, we have prayed and asked God to forgive our sins and have asked that His Son, the Lord Jesus Christ, be our Savior. It is this faith that gives us eternal life in Heaven.

A couple of days ago, I was having lunch with my pastor, and he talked about how short our physical life on Earth is. Our eternal life is forever, but our physical presence is very short. Being here physically for such a short period highlights the importance of personal forgiveness and personal grace.

When you sin, forgive yourself and give yourself grace just as God gives us His grace. The Bible tells us:

> *For as high as the heavens are above the earth, so great is his love for those who fear him; as far as the east is from the west, so far has he removed our transgressions from us. As a father has compassion on his children, so the Lord has compassion on those who fear him; for he knows how we are formed, he remembers that we are dust. For as high as the heavens are above the earth, so great is his love for those who fear him; as far as the east is from the west, so far has he removed our transgressions from us. As a father has compassion on his children, so the Lord has compassion on those who fear him; for he knows how we are formed, he remembers that we are dust. (Psalm 103:11–14)*

Everyone makes mistakes in life. My mistakes and my sins are no different than anyone else's. God does not have a sin meter that measures one sin against another. We are sinners and our sins of the past do not matter for today. Today is today and we cannot change the past. God has forgiven you. Give yourself the same "undeserved favor" and grace that God does.

A friend of mine was going through a substance abuse program at a transitional home. When it was time to leave, he was going to move out of state and away from his support group to live with family members. He said, "I am not afraid of where I am going, but I am afraid of what I am leaving." The transitional home where he had lived brought him to God and saved his life. Since I have known him, he has always been a little hard on his past mistakes. We probably all are. It does not do any good to say things like, "I messed up my life, I should have stopped or why did I do that, etc." We are sinners and, remember, God does not have a sin meter. I pray that over time, my friend can give himself more grace. We all need to give ourselves more grace.

Childhood trauma has created many of the problems we see today. Parental abuse, which can be physical, emotional, or sexual, imprints deep feelings of low self-esteem and self-worth in a child and those feelings may not go away as an adult. For those fortunate to rise above the trauma because of their faith in God, remember that, through no fault of your own, you were put in a situation you had no control over. Your abuser was most likely abused, too.

If you have not dealt with your trauma, consider making Jesus Christ your Lord and Savior and seek counsel to help you begin to heal and give yourself grace.

God and your faith will be your guide. You were the one abused. Your abuser was the sinner. Forgive the sinner and be sure to give yourself grace for what is in your past.

My friend does have God as his Savior, and with God as his Savior he will have everlasting life. He will live with God for eternity. He has the most important thing anyone of us can have in life: "faith." It does not matter what was in our past.

I would like to pray for my friend:

God, please give my friend the strength to forgive himself and give himself grace.

God, please give my friend the strength to forgive his abuser.

God, please give my friend the strength to start his new life and rebuild family relationships.

God, please give my friend the strength to remain sober as he builds his new support group.

God, please give my friend the strength to realize that the past is the past and that his faith in You will lead him to everlasting life with You, our Father.

Thank You,
God, for Your grace, and the everlasting life You give.

In Your name, with our eternal love,
Amen

Psalm 32:5, NIV

Then I acknowledged my sin to you
and did not cover up my iniquity.
I said, "I will confess
my transgressions to the Lord."
And you forgave
the guilt of my sin.

Matthew 21:21–22, NIV

Jesus replied, "Truly I tell you, if you have faith and do not doubt,
not only can you do what was done to the fig tree,
but also you can say to this mountain,
'Go, throw yourself in the sea', and it will be done.
If you believe, you will receive whatever you ask for in prayer."

My Prayer for All Who Are Seeking the Grace of God

Dear God,

When I first came to You, I did not understand what Your grace meant. Studying Your Word has given me an understanding of what it means when You give us grace. Thank You, God, for the grace You give Your children. Please help all those seeking You to understand Your grace. The grace You provide is an example of the grace we need to provide others. We need to recognize that, as hard as we try, we will sin. When we sin and ask for Your forgiveness, it is Your grace that forgives our sins. We need to give ourselves the same grace that You give us and forgive ourselves when we sin. We need to give others the same grace that You give us and forgive them when they sin against us. Your grace is healing to us and the grace we provide others is healing to them.

God, please help those who do not understand Your grace. Please help them know that You are a forgiving God. It is Your forgiveness that helps us journey forward to further press into Your Word and further understand the love You have for us. I pray for those seeking You and pray that they can learn from Your grace, heal, and move forward in their lives.

"My Lord and my God!" John 21:28, NIV

Your loving and devoted son,
Amen

1. Why do we deserve God's grace or undeserved favor?

2. God forgives us for our sins and gives us His grace. Is it hard for you to give yourself the same undeserved favor that God gives us?

3. We know that we are sinners and not perfect. Does this make you feel inadequate in the eyes of God? Why or why not?

4. Think about a time in your life when someone caused you to have feelings of low self-esteem and self-worth. How can your love of God and the grace He provides help you to overcome this emotional abuse and live in your true identity as His beloved child?

WORSHIP MUSIC RECOMMENDATIONS

Amazing Grace • Taya Smith
youtube.com/watch?v=1E_7WyiDF7U

Holy Water • We the Kingdom
youtube.com/watch?v=7KLQ2AXQmtA&list=RD7KLQ2AXQmtA&start_radio=1 

I AM

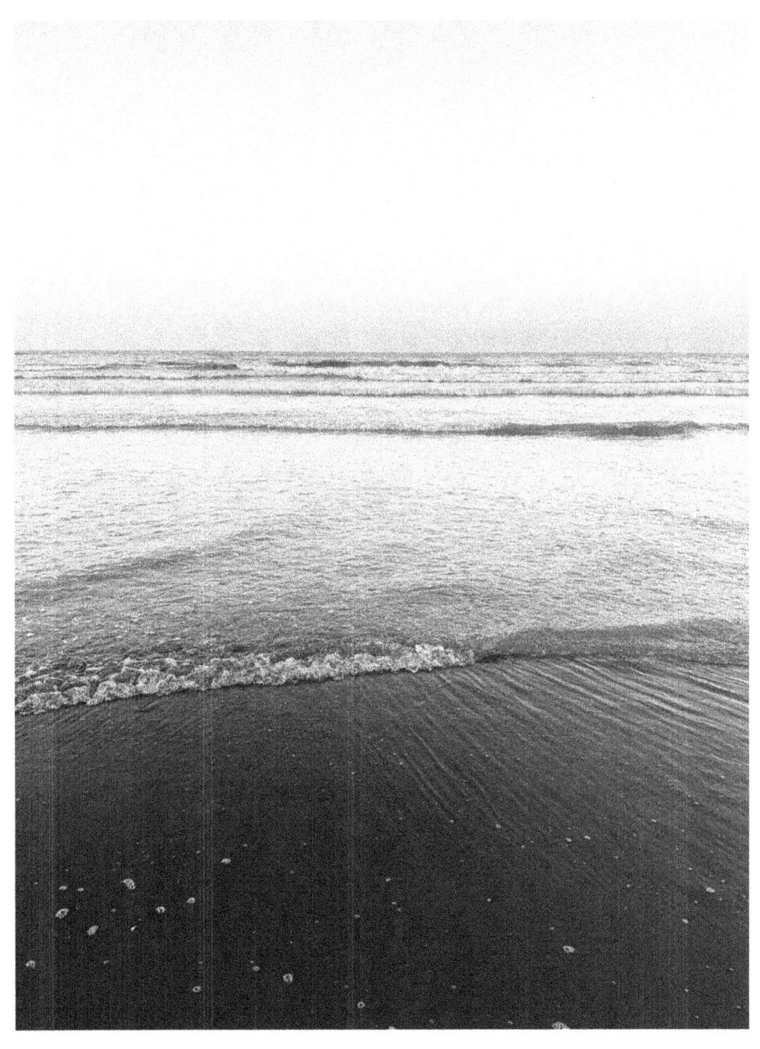

I AM
PART I

A Poem

"I AM" IS A SERIES of short poems based on Jesus's "I Am" verses in the Bible. Each "I Am" verse in the Bible is followed by a statement. There are seven "I Am" verses and they occur only in the book of John, in chapters 6 through 15.

Jesus spoke the first "I Am" verse in the spring of AD 29 and the seventh verse a year later in the spring of AD 30, which was shortly before His crucifixion. Jesus's location when He made the "I Am" statements ranged from Gennesaret on the western side of the Sea of Galilee to Bethany and Jerusalem. It is believed that the second "I Am" statement occurred during the Festival of the Tabernacles on the temple grounds in Jerusalem. The final two "I Am" verses, John 14:6 and John 15:1, were at the Last Supper. When reading the Jesus's "I Am" verses, I like to think, **"He Is"**:

"He Is" the Bread of Life.

"He Is" the Light of the World.

"He Is" the Gate for the Sheep.

"He Is" the Good Shepherd.

"He Is" the Resurrection and the Life.

"He Is" the Way and the Truth and the Life.

"He Is" the True Vine.

"He Is" the only way to eternal life with our Father. "He Is" our Lord and Savior, and "He Is" the one who died so our sins would forever be forgiven.

2 Corinthians 5:21, NIV
God made him who had no sin to be sin for us,
so that in him we might become the righteousness of God.

The first and second "I Am" statements are"

"I Am the Bread of Life" (John 6:35, NIV)

and

"I Am the Light of the World" (John 8:12, NIV)

They are about why the Father sent Jesus and why He is here. They are about faith and following Jesus and God's "Way," and that following Jesus and God's Way will bring eternal life and spiritual food forever. Shortly after Jesus says, "I Am the Light of the World," He was challenged by the Pharisees for referring to Himself as "I Am."

John 8:58, NIV
"Very truly I tell you," Jesus answered, "before Abraham was born, I am!"
At this, they picked up stones to stone him, but Jesus hid himself,
slipping away from the temple grounds.

Prior to Jesus referencing Himself as "I Am," the "I Am" statement had only been used by God when Moses asked God how he should reference God to the Israelites, and God replied,

Exodus 3:14, NIV

"I AM WHO I AM. This is what you are to say to the Israelites: 'I AM has sent me to you.'"

I AM THE BREAD OF LIFE

I am the road to salvation

I am your water for thirst

I am the faith for your journey

I was sent to be first

Come to me

Come with your faith

It is my Father's will

Believe in his fate

I feed the 5000

And will feed 5000 more

Believers in me

Will be hungry no more

Then Jesus declared,"I am the bread of life.Whoever comes to me will never go hungry, and whoever believes in me will never be thirsty. But as I told you, you have seen me and you still do not believe. All those the Father gives me will come to me, and whoever comes to me I will never drive away. For I have come down from heaven not to do my will but to do the will of him who sent me. And this is the will of him who sent me, that I shall lose none of all those he has given me, but raise them up at the last day. For my Father's will is that everyone who looks to the Son and believes in him shall have eternal life, and I will raise them up at the last day."

I AM THE LIGHT OF THE WORLD

Come in from the dark
I know where to go
My light is your path
Your faith makes it so

My witness is Father
For I witness too
He sent me to save
To make believers of you

I know where I come
And I know where I go
But you question, "I Am"
And the truth that I sow

John 8:12–18

When Jesus spoke again to the people, he said, "I am the light of the world.
Whoever follows me will never walk in darkness, but will have the light of life."
The Pharisees challenged him, "Here you are, appearing as your own witness; your testimony is not valid."
Jesus answered, "Even if I testify on my own behalf, my testimony is valid, for I know where I come from
and where I am going. But you have no idea where I come from or where I am going. You judged by human
standards; I pass judgement on no one. But if I do judge, my decisions are true, because I am not alone.
I stand with the Father, who sent me. In your own Law it is written that the testimony of two witnesses is true.
I am one who testifies for myself; my other witness is the Father, who sent me."

In the third and fourth "I Am" statements,

"I Am the Gate for the Sheep" (John 10:7, NIV)

and

"I Am the Good Shepherd" (John 10:11, NIV),

Jesus compares Himself to an actual gate and then to a shepherd. In saying He is "the gate for the sheep," He is illustrating that the only way into Heaven, to the Father's home, is through His Father's gate and that there are no other gates. All other beliefs come from "thieves and robbers." There is only one God, one gate and one Way.

The Scripture verse, "I am the good shepherd," occurs twice: first in John 10:11 and second in John 10:14. In comparing Himself to a shepherd, Jesus is saying that we are the sheep and that the sheep must follow the shepherd. A shepherd leads his flock, a shepherd will guard his flock, and a shepherd will lay down his life for his flock. The flock knows the shepherd and the flock has faith in the shepherd. In John 10:15, Jesus predicts His death by stating that a shepherd will lay down his life for the sheep.

John 10:15, NIV

"I lay down my life for the sheep."

Jesus also states in John 10:16 that His flock is open to all, including the Gentiles, and that the flock will grow:

"I have other sheep that are not all of this sheep pen. I must bring them also. They too will listen to my voice, and there shall be one flock and one shepherd."

I AM THE GATE FOR THE SHEEP

Come in through the gate

The "Way" is for you

Follow the herder

And forever ensues

A pasture of green

A flock that will follow

The "Word" is my crook

And a love that's not hollow

Before Me they came

But their lies are not true

The "Way" is my gate

And it's open to you

John 10:7–10, NIV

Therefore Jesus said again, "Very truly I tell you, I am the gate for the sheep.

All who come before me are thieves and robbers, but the sheep have not listened to them.

I am the gate; whoever enters through me will be saved.

They will come in and go out, and find pasture.

The thief comes only to steal and kill and destroy;

I have come that they may have life,

and have it to the full.

I AM THE GOOD SHEPHERD

The good Shepherd, "I Am"

Sent by Father for all

To watch over the flock

No lamb is too small

But wolves prey on weakness

And sin is forever

Father's Word is salvation

And His love is forever

I gather more sheep

But My life will be given

Unbridled love for Father

For His flock is in Heaven

John 10:11–18, NIV

"I am the good shepherd. The good shepherd lays down his life for the sheep. The hired hand is not the shepherd and does not own the sheep. So when he sees the wolf coming, he abandons the sheep and runs away. Then the wolf attacks the flock and scatters it. The man runs away because he is a hired hand and care nothing for the sheep."

"I am the good shepherd; I know my sheep and my sheep know me—just as the Father knows me and I know the Father—and I lay down my life for the sheep. I have other sheep that are not of this sheep pen. I must bring them also. They too will listen to my voice, and there shall be one flock and one shepherd. The reason my Father loves me is that I lay down my life—only to take it up again. No one takes it from me, but I lay it down of my own accord. I have authority to lay it down and authority to take it up again. This command I receive from my Father."

Psalm 23, NIV

The Lord is my shepherd, I lack nothing.
He makes me lie down in green pastures,
he leads me beside quiet waters,
he refreshes my soul.

He guides me along the right paths
for his name's sake.
Even though I walk
through the darkest valley,
I will fear no evil,
for you are with me;
your rod and your staff,
they comfort me.

You prepare a table for me
in the presence of my enemies.
You anoint my head with oil;
my cup overflows.

Surely your goodness and love will follow me
all the days of my life,
and I will dwell in the house of the Lord
forever.

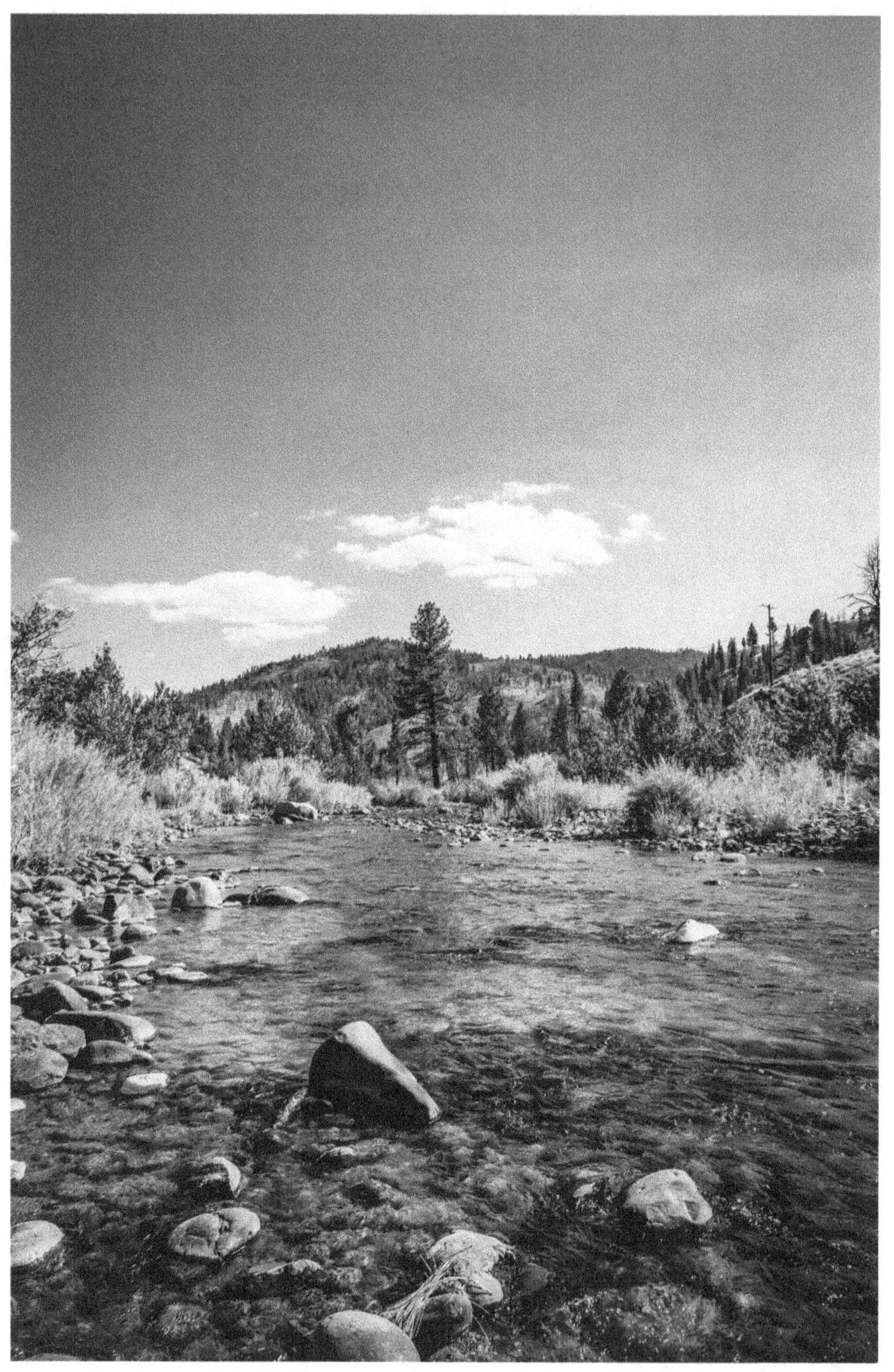

My Prayer to "I Am," for Very Truly "He Is"

Dear God,

Please give me the strength to fully understand what You have done for us by sending us Your Son, Jesus, who was pure and sinless, to die for us so we could live forever. He became sin so our sins would forever be forgiven, and we could live with You for eternity. Please give me the strength to fully understand what the crucifixion of Your Son means. He is the Way; He is Eternal Life. He died so I could live. He is my Savior and the Lord of my life.

Five years ago, when I prayed and came back to You, giving my heart to You, I did not fully understand what sending Your Son to die for our sins truly meant. Your Son is my Savior; Your Son is my Lord. Thank You for sending Your Son and sending Yourself so we could be saved. You and Your Son are very truly "I Am."

"My Lord and my God!" John 21:28, NIV

Your loving and devoted son,
Amen

Reflections for Your Spiritual Journey

1. What does each of the first four "I Am" verses mean to you and your relationship with our Lord and Savior Jesus Christ?

2. Read Psalm 23 again (above). What are the primary responsibilities of a shepherd? How do you see them in this passage?

3. If Jesus Christ is your Lord and Savior, and your shepherd, what are your responsibilities as a sheep in the flock?

4. Jesus also compares Himself to a gate (John 10:7–10, above). How is He the gate to the Kingdom of God and eternal (abundant) life? Do you know how to access that gate? Have you?

<hr>

WORSHIP MUSIC RECOMMENDATIONS

 *Daily Bread* • Pat Barrett and Kari Jobe
youtube.com/watch?v=zWt4-_UKM5U&list=RDzWt4-_UKM5U&start_radio=1

Light of the World • Lauren Daigle
youtube.com/watch?v=_cLhaZIBSpo 

I AM
PART II

A Poem

"He is" the Resurrection and the Life.

"He is" the Way and the Truth and the Life.

"He is" the True Vine.

IN JESUS'S SHORT MINISTRY, He knew whom He wanted to travel with, i.e., His disciples, His chosen apostles (note: "apostle" means "sent-out one"). He knew where He wanted to go and which groups of people He wanted to minister to. He was very selective in how and when He would perform a miracle. His first miracle was when He turned water into wine at the wedding that His mother Mary was attending (John chapter 2). His last miracle occurred after His resurrection at the Sea of Galilee, when He appeared to Peter, Thomas, Nathanael, and some other disciples. The disciples had gone fishing the night before and had caught nothing. Then Jesus appeared:

John 21:5–7, NIV

He called out to them, "Friends, haven't you any fish?"

"No," they answered.

He said, "Throw your net on the right side of the boat and you will find some."

When they did this, they were unable to haul the net in because of the large number of fish.

Then the disciple whom Jesus loved said to Peter, "It is the Lord!"

Performing miracles was one way Jesus would show the Jews and the Gentiles that He was sent by God and that He was the Messiah.

When Jesus resurrected Lazarus from the grave, in John 11:43, He was using this miracle as a symbol of the resurrection of our own lives, and as a symbol of His own resurrection. This miracle and the related scriptures were Jesus's way to show His disciples of His coming death and His resurrection that would follow. He also knew that this miracle would cause the Jewish leaders to work with the Romans in hopes of ordering His crucifixion.

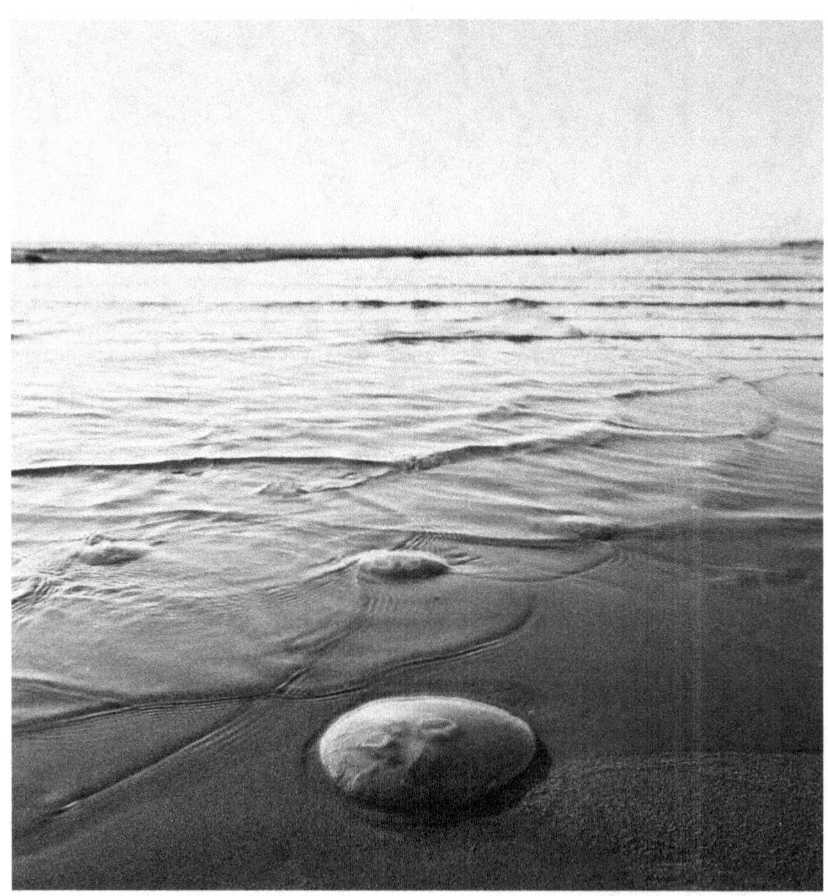

The fifth "I Am" verse is:

"I Am the Resurrection and the Life." (John 11:25, NIV)

It was made directly to Lazarus's sister, Martha. Lazarus had died four days earlier and had already been put in a tomb and wrapped in strips of linen. When Jesus arrived in Bethany, in a conversation He was having with Martha where she was referring to her brother's death, she said, in John 11:24, "I know he will rise again in the resurrection at the last day."

Jesus replied to Martha,

John 11:25–26, NIV

"I Am the Resurrection and the Life. The one who believes in me will live, even though they die; and who lives by believing in me will never die. Do you believe this?"

Martha replied to Jesus,

John 11:27, NIV

"Yes, Lord…I believe that you are the Messiah, the son of God, who is to come into the world."

Jesus then resurrected Lazarus from his tomb:

John 11:40–44, NIV

Then Jesus said, "Did I not tell that if you believe, you will see the glory of God?"
So they took away the stone. Then Jesus looked up and said, "Father, I thank you that you have heard me. I knew that you always hear me, but I said this for the benefit of the people standing here, that they may believe that you sent me." When he said this, Jesus called out in a loud voice, "Lazarus, come out!"
The dead man came out, his hands and feet wrapped with strips of linen,
and a cloth around his face. Jesus said to them, "Take off the grave clothes and let him go."

I AM THE RESURRECTION AND THE LIFE

Believe in Me
To resurrect your beginning
Life eternal
Life free from sinning

She believed in Me
"Son of God" as was written
It is My time for this world
I ask that faith will be given

I'll be crucified to rise
But your faith is still hollow
As Lazarus knows
Your faith is to follow

The sixth "I Am" verse occurred at the Last Supper:

"I Am the Way and the Truth and the Life." (John 14:6, NIV)

Many of Jesus's words in John 14 are statements to the apostles reinforcing that, by knowing Jesus, they know the Father. The verses are preparing the apostles for the ministry that is ahead of them, because Jesus will be leaving them soon.

John 14:7, NIV

"If you really know me, you will know my Father as well. From now on, you do know him and have seen him."

John 14:12, NIV

"Very truly I tell you, whoever believes in me will do the works I have been doing, and they will do even greater things than these, because I am going to the Father."

I AM THE WAY AND THE TRUTH AND THE LIFE

Come to Me

To see the Father I know

And in knowing Me

You'll know where to go

But you question My Way

And the path that I've shown

You say, "Show me the Father"

And then you'll come home

But in knowing Me

You will know Father too

And the gifts that I have

I give freely to you

John 14:6–14

Jesus answered, "I am the way and the truth and the life.

No one comes to the Father except through me.

If you really know me, you will know my Father as well.

From now on, you do know him and have seen him."

Philip said, "Lord, show us the Father and that will be enough for us."

Jesus answered: "Don't you know me, Philip, even after I have been among you such a long time?

Anyone who has seen me has seen the Father.

How can you say, 'Show us the Father?'

Don't you believe that I am in the Father, and that the Father is in me?

The words I say to you I do not speak in my own authority.

Rather, it is the Father, living in me, who is doing the work.

Believe me when I say that I am in the Father and the Father is in me;

or at least believe in the evidence of the works themselves.

Very truly I tell you, whoever believes in me will do the works I have been doing,

and they will do even greater things than these, because I am going to the Father.

And I will do whatever you ask in my name,

so that the Father may be glorified in the Son.

You may ask me for anything in my name, and I will do it."

The seventh and final "I Am" verse also occurred at the Last Supper":

"I Am the True Vine." (John 15:1, NIV)

Jesus compares Himself to a vine. He is the vine; we are the branches and the Father is the Gardener. Branches from the vine must be pruned so the remaining branches will be more plentiful and yield more fruit. Also, no branch can bear fruit by itself, and fruitful branches must remain in the vine.

John 15:5, NIV
"I am the vine; you are the branches. If you remain in me and I in you,
you will bear much fruit; apart from me you can do nothing."

I AM THE TRUE VINE

Remain in Me
For the fruit of the vine
A vine grown by Father
Yielding fruit for all time

Some branches are fruitless
And need to be pruned
But all branches need vines
For the vine helps them bloom

When branches bear fruit
And we remain together
Father's vine will be nourished
And His Way is forever

John 15:1–4

"I am the true vine, and my Father is the gardener.

He cuts off every branch in me that bears no fruit,

while every branch that does bear fruit he prunes so that it will be even more fruitful.

You are already clean because of the word I have spoken to you.

Remain in me, as I also remain in you.

No branch can bear fruit by itself; it must remain in the vine.

Neither can you bear fruit unless you remain in me.

I am the vine; you are the branches.

If you remain in me and I in you, you will bear much fruit;

apart from me you can do nothing.

If you do not remain in me, you are like a branch that is thrown away and withers;

such branches are picked up, thrown into the fire and burned.

If you remain in me and my words remain in you,

ask whatever you wish, and it will be done for you.

This is to my Father's glory, that you bear much fruit, showing yourself to be disciples."

The final poem in this chapter is called "I Am Who I Am." It is about God referring to Himself as "I Am" in Exodus 3:14. Moses asked God how he should reference God to the Israelites. God replied,

"I AM WHO I AM. This is what you are to say to the Israelites: 'I AM has sent me to you.'" (Exodus 3:14, NIV)

To quote the final stanza in the poem:

"Let light shine from darkness

And darkness be light

I am the Creator of all

The 'I AM' that brings life"

God was first. God was in the beginning. God is the beginning. He sent His Son to be our Savior. There are two persons but they are ONE. God is *"I Am"* and His Son is *"I Am."*

"I Am"… is One.

God and His Son are *"I Am,"* but to us, God and His Son *Very Truly Are.*

"He Is."

"He Is" our Savior. "He Is" the one who died for us. "He Is" the one who bears our sin. "He Is" the one who shows us the Way. "He Is" the one who is preparing our eternal home and "He Is" the one who will return. Love and worship "He Is" with all your heart. Bare your soul, never be afraid, and always have faith.

"He Is" your "I Am."

I AM WHO I AM

I am who I am

I made it so

I come from the past

So long, long ago

But the past is the present

And time will suspend

Light is eternal

And life will not end

I am here from afar

To bring in the light

I am here from afar

To make darkness so bright

Let light shine from darkness

And darkness be light

I am the Creator of all

The "I Am" that brings life

Exodus 3:13–15

Moses said to God, "Suppose I go to Israelites and say to them,

"The God of your fathers has sent me, and they ask me,

'What is his name?' Then what shall I tell them?"

God said to Moses, "I AM WHO I AM.

This is what you are to say to the Israelites: 'I AM has sent me to you.'"

God also said to Moses, "Say to the Israelites, 'THE LORD, the God of your fathers—

the God of Abraham, the God of Isaac and the God of Jacob—has sent me to you.'

This is my name forever, the name you shall call me from generation to generation."

Revelation 21:6–7, NIV

He said to me: "It is done. I am the Alpha and the Omega, the Beginning and the End.

To the thirsty I will give water without cost from the spring of the water of life.

Those who are victorious will inherit all this, and I will be their God and they will be my children."

Genesis 15:1, NIV

After this, the word of the Lord came to Abram in a vision:

"Do not be afraid, Abram.

I am your shield,

your very great reward."

My Prayer to "I Am," for Very Truly "He Is"

Dear God,

When I read the "I Am" verses, I need to think "He Is." Your Son, Jesus Christ, is my Bread, my Light, my Gate to You, my Shepherd, my Resurrection to eternal life, the Way, and my Vine.

The seven "I Am" verses show me how unconditional Your love is. You sent Your Son to die so I could live. You sent Your Son to bring light into a dark world. You sent Your Son to show us the Way.

One of the recommended songs in this chapter is called "Falling in Love." Please help me, God, to continue to fall in love more and more with Your Son. Please help me to better understand the unconditional love You and Your Son have for me. And please help me to continue every day to go deeper and deeper in Your Word so I can better understand Your Way and the love You have for me. Jesus Christ is my Lord and Shepherd. I know I have His unconditional love. Please help me return to Him the same unconditional love He provides to me.

"My Lord and my God!" John 21:28, NIV

Your loving and devoted son,
Amen

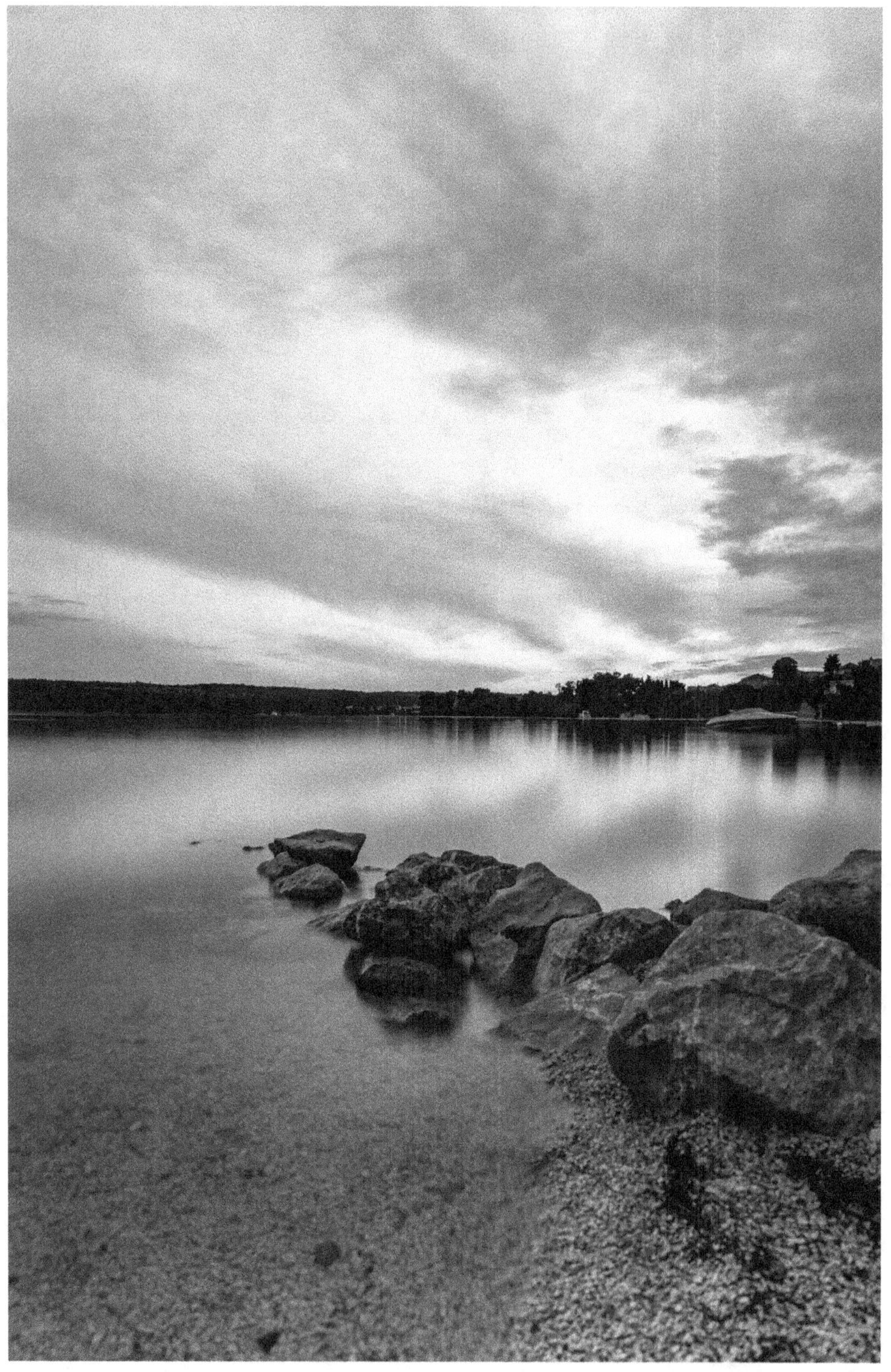

Reflections for Your Journey

1. In the fifth "I Am" verse, Jesus states that He is the resurrection of life. In John 11:49–50, the Jewish high priest, Caiaphas, says, "You know nothing at all! You do not realize that it is better for you that one man die for the people than that the whole nation perish." Why do you think the Jewish leader feared that the nation would perish by believing that Jesus was the Messiah?

2. The sixth and seventh "I Am" verses occurred at the Last Supper. What message do you think Jesus was trying to give to His disciples with these final two "I Am" verses?

3. It is a great mystery that God, Jesus, and the Holy Spirit are three persons, yet One. How do you relate to God as Father? How do you relate to Jesus as the Son—and your Savior and friend? How do you relate to the Holy Spirit, whom Jesus said He would send as a "Counselor" or "Advocate" (John 14:26)?

4. After watching the worship music recommendations below, record your thoughts or prayers about who God is to you.

WORSHIP MUSIC RECOMMENDATIONS

Falling in Love • Phil Wickham
youtube.com/watch?v=gkwPy3deHtQ

What a Beautiful Name • Hillsong United
youtube.com/watch?v=nQWFzMvCfLE

THE BLESSING

THE BLESSING

IN THE END, our blessings are given to God. I give my blessing to God for inspiring me to write this book and giving me the strength to finish it. I give my blessing to God for bringing people to me who assisted and challenged me with comments on the writings. And I give my blessing to God for you, the readers that God brought to the book.

It is my hope that in reading my poems and inspirations that your belief in God our Father grows. Growing our belief and faith in God is a spiritual journey that lasts our lifetime. We are here on Earth for a very short period, and it is hard to grasp in our short stay the all-surpassing beauty of God—**God, the creator of all.**

I hope that my writings will help you look deeper into God. My writings come from personal experiences, conversations with others, and opening my eyes to God's beautiful world. All of us experience things every day that God wants us to see. Unfortunately, many times we do not stop to see what God wants us to see. For me, God has opened my eyes to His beautiful world. Each day I hope I can experience something powerful that God wants me to see. And what God wants me to see is not the same as what God wants you to see. Reflecting on the inspirational writing, "Todd's Prayer," I would point out that Todd had no idea that God was sending him to answer the prayer of the barista. Todd thought God was sending him to pray for the homeless woman.

God wants all of us to grow and learn from the experiences He puts us in. God has created a beautiful world, and our time here is limited. Enjoy each day to its fullest.

Finally, I would like to thank everyone who has spent time reading my poems and inspirations. They are very personal and meaningful to me. Your time is valuable and there are many spiritually inspirational books to read. As I grow my spiritual journey, I hope God will keep inspiring me to write and share with others.

Thank you again. I send you my blessing as you continue along your spiritual journey, growing your relationship with God our Father.

"PEACE BE WITH YOU!" (John 20:19, NIV)

John 14:1–7, NIV

"Do not let your hearts be troubled. You believe in God, believe also in me.
My Father's house has many rooms; if that were not so,
would I have told you that I am going there to prepare a place for you?
And if I go and prepare a place for you, I will come back and take you to be with me
that you also may be where I am. You know the place to where I am going."
Thomas said to him, "Lord, we do not know where you are going, so how can we know the way?"
Jesus answered, "I am the way and the truth and the life.
No one comes to the Father except through me.
If you really know me, you will know my Father as well.
From now on, you do know him and have seen him."

WORSHIP MUSIC RECOMMENDATIONS

The Blessing • Cody Carnes and Kari Jobe, Elevation Worship
youtube.com/watch?v=Zp6aygmvzM4

I Won't Let Your Song Go Unsung • Jenn Bostic
youtube.com/watch?v=LW_ESPxjQ3U

Way Maker • Leeland
youtube.com/watch?v=iJCV_2H9xD0

APPENDIX

CONVERSATION

"CONVERSATION" WAS ONE of the first poems I ever wrote. Unfortunately, I do not remember exactly when I wrote it but I do remember that it was shortly after I proposed to my wife, which was fall quarter of our senior year in college. Because we were still in school and we both had internships after graduation, our engagement lasted over a year and a half.

"Conversation" was my "wedding vow" to Cathy. We were married on March 26, 1983. The poem was read a second time when we renewed our wedding vows on our thirty-eighth wedding anniversary. Poems like this are not read very often. Maybe they should be? Each time I read the poem, the words and meaning get stronger. A strong marriage and a marriage that endures all the challenges of life takes work. As the poem says,

> *"Love takes time and, when found, requires work,*
> *Effort, and a commitment so as not to be lost."*

How our lives unfold is unpredictable. So many events in our lives are not under our control. But we can control how we treat others, especially the ones we love. The work and commitment we put into relationships with the ones we love yield rewards and blessings that make our lives fulfilled.

On March 26, 2022, I read Cathy a second poem I wrote her for our thirty-ninth wedding anniversary. It is called "Conversation 2022." It reflects back on our thirty-nine years of marriage and how the commitments we made at our wedding have given us the strength to work through and endure all the challenges of life. As the poem "Conversation" says,

> *"My friend, you are right; I am a lucky man."*

I thank God for all my blessings and for bringing me a partner, a soulmate, and the Love of my Life.

CONVERSATION

I thought I would buy her a gift.

Why?

Do you think she needed it to reassure her of your love,

or did you need it to reassure yourself of your love?

No, just a present, because she is special.

Special?

You mean a gifted woman,

or do you mean someone who holds a special place in your heart?

She holds my whole heart.

You see my friend, I've become very attached to that woman.

I feel her warmth radiating from her smile.

We laugh and share the times, we cry and share the tears, and we love and share the hope.

You see my friend, I love that woman.

Do you love that woman?

She must be very special then.

Love takes time and, when found, requires work, effort, and a commitment

so as not to be lost.

Love is a feeling, an emotion, capable of acting "*off-the-cuff*," irrational and unpredictable.

But love holds rewards that are eternal, rewards never lost to memory.

I am ready.

For what?
To make the commitment?

To feel the love, to retain the love, to love the love.
I am not in love with only love itself.
I love a woman who is tender and soft,
whose life is living and love is giving.
You see, my friend, that woman loves me and would do anything for me.

You are a lucky man.

Very true.
I sometimes take advantage of the love,
but I would be lost without it.
I don't want to lose that woman.
She is my smile, my hope and my encouragement.
My friend, you are right; I am a lucky man.

Good-bye.
Good-bye, my friend.
(1983)

CONVERSATION 2022

Hello, my friend.

Do you realize that it has been thirty-nine years since we have spoken?

Hello to you.

I hope you have had a good life?

The last time we spoke you were going to marry a woman you loved very much

I hope you two have had a wonderful life?

We have.

She is as beautiful today as she was thirty-nine years ago.

She is such a kind and loving person.

As I said thirty-nine years ago, "She is a very special woman."

Congratulations.

I remember telling you that "love takes time and, when found, requires work, effort,

and a commitment to not be lost,"

and that "love holds rewards that are eternal."

How has your marriage gone?

We have two beautiful grown girls whom we are very proud of.

They have two kind and caring men in their lives.

We both are healthy and are looking forward to our retirement years.

But there have been some problems.

What would they be?

Selfishness from me.

My selfishness makes me hard to live with.

My selfishness led me to infidelity.

My selfishness led me to financial ruin.

And with my selfishness, I almost lost the woman I love.

Did this go on through much of your marriage?

Any amount of time is too long.

I wasn't kind and I have not been fair.

I forgot my beautiful wedding vows.

And, I forgot what the most important thing in my life is…her.

I forgot what I said thirty-nine years ago to you:

"To feel the love, to retain the love, to love the love.

I am not in love with only love itself.

I love a woman who is tender and soft,

whose life is living and love is giving.

You see my friend, that woman loves me and would do anything for me."

That is what I forgot.

Are you still that same person?

No…Two years ago we brought God into our lives.

Have you confessed your sins to God?

Have you confessed your sins to your wife?

Yes…I am healing, my friend.

We are both healing.

Bringing God into our lives has brought beautiful changes to our marriage.

I believe God has worked a miracle for us.

That is what God does.

He works miracles.

God only wants His children to be happy.

We are His children and any parent wants their children to be happy.

Yes, that is what we feel.

We both love God and we are building our own relationship with Him.

It is so amazing, building our marriage with God by our side.

At night, I hold my cross and thank God for the beautiful woman by my side.

Remember to be kind to each other.

Remember to be faithful to each other.

Remember to be honest to each other.

And do not forget what you learn from God's Word…It is "The Word."

Yes…we are learning so much everyday about "The Word."

Thank you, my friend, for still being here.

Thirty-nine years is a long time.

I hope to talk to you again soon.

Remember what I said to you thirty-nine years ago:

"You are a lucky man."

I am…a very lucky man.

Good-bye, my friend.

Good-bye.

(March 26, 2022)

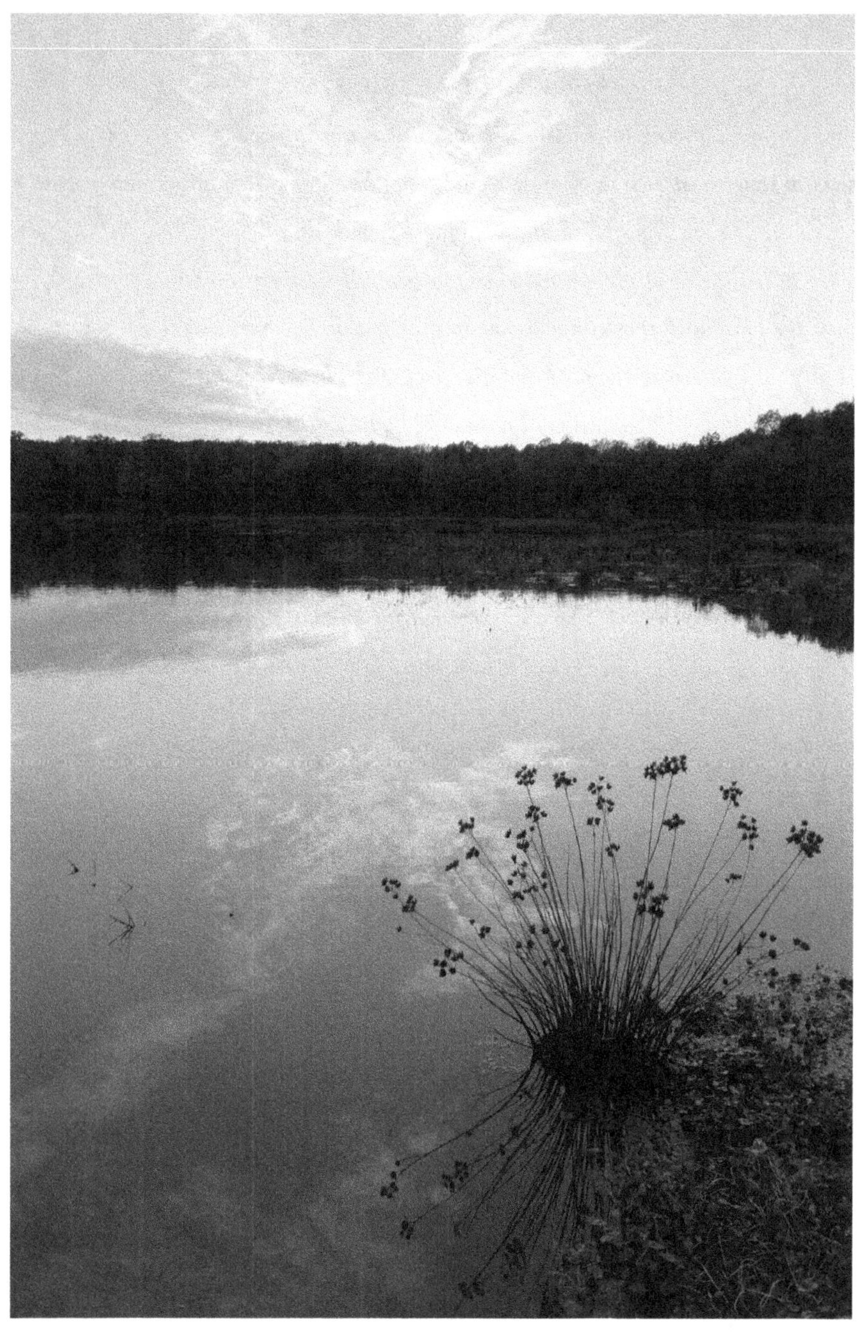

1 CORINTHIANS 13:1–8, NIV

And yet I will show you the most excellent way.

If I speak in tongues of men or of angels, but do not have love, I am only a resounding gong

or a clanging cymbal.

If I have the gift of prophecy and can fathom all mysteries and all knowledge,

and If I have faith that can move mountains, but do not have love, I am nothing.

If I give all I possess to the poor and give over my body to hardship that I may boast,

but do not have love, I gain nothing.

Love is patient, love is kind. It does not envy, it does boast, it is not proud.

It does not dishonor others, it is not self-seeking, it is not easily angered, it keeps no record of wrongs.

Love does not delight in evil but rejoices with the truth.

It always protects, always trusts, always hopes, always perseveres.

Love never fails.

My Prayer for All Who Are Married or Soon to Be Married

Dear God,

You provide us with many gifts. The first gift You have given us is Your Son. Accepting Your Son as our Lord and Savior provides us with salvation and eternal life with You. The second gift You provide for us is our life. We live because of You, and we live for You.

Another gift is the gift of marriage. If we choose to accept that gift, we are also given the opportunity to bless You and bless ourselves with the gift of children. It is amazing what You provide for us when we accept the gift of marriage.

Thank You for bringing me an amazing partner. She is the rock to our foundation. And thank You for bringing us two amazing children. I pray that You watch over them and bless them with marriages built on Your foundation, and provide for them the amazing gift of children, too.

I pray that all who are married or are soon to be married will understand Your Word and the Scriptures as they are written. I pray they will commit to each other as You have commanded us, as lifelong partners.

Thank You, God, for the gift of Your Son. Thank You for my life, thank You for bringing me my partner and wife, and thank You for blessing us with children. As I say in the poem "Conversation," "I am a lucky man."

In Your name,
Your loving and devoted son,
Amen

WORSHIP MUSIC RECOMMENDATIONS

Thank God • Kane Brown

youtube.com/watch?v=bLzUmfLckEw

ABOUT THE AUTHOR

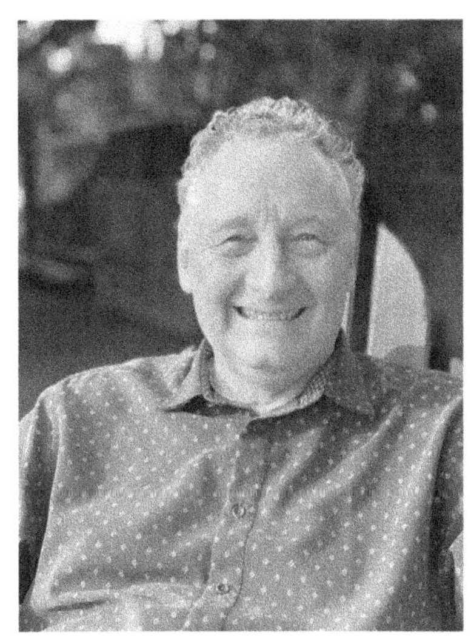

L. Brien Elvins was born and raised in Tacoma, Washington. He grew up in a strong Christian family, but as a young teenager he stopped attending church. After his children were born, he started to casually seek out God, but did not find the avenue to rebuild his faith. Five years prior to writing this book, a friend—who is a strong Christian—asked him a couple of times to give his heart to God. The answer was, "No, I am fine." But finally, the answer was, "Yes."

Within a couple of months after making Jesus Christ His Lord and Savior, Brien started to write stories and poetry to personally document His return to our Lord. The writing and poetry evolved and, after receiving many positive comments from family and friends, he embarked on the journey to write *Born Again: The Journey Begins—One Man's Walk with God.*

Brien graduated from the University of Washington and has spent his professional career in the Financial Services industry. He and his wife Cathy have two wonderful daughters and one granddaughter. He enjoys time at home and his project is making a mid-century-modern home "modern" again. He also feels blessed to have so many good friends and family members in the area with whom he can spend quality time and celebrate the goodness of God.

www.bornagainthejourneybegins.com